PERPLEXITIES AND PARADOXES

PERPLEXITIES AND PARADOXES

by

MIGUEL UNAMUNO

*Translated from the Spanish
by Stuart Gross*

GREENWOOD PRESS, PUBLISHERS
WESTPORT, CONNECTICUT

TABLE OF CONTENTS

My Religion 1

Concerning Public Opinion 10

Civilization is Civism 14

From the Correspondence of a Fighter 22

Writers and the People 28

Politics and Culture 36

Hispanic Envy 42

Ibsen and Kierkegaard 51

The Moral Urge 58

Truth and Life 67

The Spanish Christ 75

Rascal and Scat 81

The Portico of the Temple 89

Fanatical Scepticism 95

On Obscenity 102

Popular Materialism 109

Don Juan Tenorio 118

Pseudoscience 127

Three Generations 136

On Lust 143

Naturalness 150

The Song of Eternal Waters 154

To a Young Writer 160

My Religion

A friend writes me from Chile saying that people there keep asking him this question, "Briefly, what is Mr. Unamuno's religion?" As this is not the first time I have been confronted with such a question, I am going to attempt, not to answer it, but to clarify the meaning of the question.

Peoples as well as individuals who are spiritually lazy —and spiritual laziness is wedded to extreme economic activity — whether they know it or not, desire it or not, seek it or not, lean toward dogmatism. Spiritual laziness flees from a critical or skeptical attitude.

I say skeptical, but taking the term skepticism in its etymological and philosophical sense, because skeptic means not one who doubts but one who investigates or searches carefully, as contrasted with one who affirms and believes that he has found out. There are those who scrutinize a problem, and there are those who give us a formula, whether it's the right one or not, as its solution.

In the realm of pure philosophical speculation it is precipitant to ask one for an exact solution, provided that he has furthered the clarification of a problem. When a long calculation turns out to be wrong, erasing what has been done and beginning again represents substantial progress. When a house threatens to fall or becomes completely uninhabitable, we tear it down, and we can't

1

insist that another be built on its foundations. It is possible to build a new one with materials from the old, but only after tearing down the old one. Meanwhile the people can take refuge in a hut, if they don't have another house, or sleep in the open.

And we must not lose sight of the fact that in our daily life we rarely have to wait for definite scientific solutions. Men have lived, and still do, by hypotheses and very frail explanations, and even without any. In chastising a criminal, men don't stop to agree as to whether or not he had free will, just as in sneezing one doesn't reflect about the harm that may come to him from the little obstacle in his throat that precipitates the sneeze.

To do them justice, I believe that men who maintain that if they didn't believe in the eternal punishment of hell they would sin, are mistaken. If they were to stop believing in penalties beyond the grave, not for this reason would they grow worse. They would merely seek another ideal justification for their conduct. The person who, being good, believes in a transcendental order, is not good so much because he believes in it as he believes in it because he is good. That this proposition will appear obscure and nonsensical to the over-inquisitive who are spiritually lazy, I am certain.

And I shall be asked, "What is your religion?" and I shall answer that my religion is to seek truth in life and life in truth, conscious that I shall not find them while I live; my religion is to struggle tirelessly and incessantly with the unknown; my religion is to struggle with God as they say Jacob did from earliest dawn until nightfall. I shall not admit the Unknowable and the

Unrecognizable of which pedants write, nor any, "beyond this thou shalt not pass." I reject any eternal *ignorabimus*. In any event I wish to reach the inaccessible.

"Be perfect as your Father in Heaven is perfect," Christ said to us, and such an ideal of perfection is, beyond any doubt, unattainable. But He set the unattainable as the goal of our efforts. And he filled the gap, say the theologians, by supplying grace. I want to fight my battle without preoccupying myself about the victory. Are there not armies and even peoples headed for sure defeat? Do we not praise those who die fighting rather than surrender? Well, this is my religion.

Those who ask me this question are seeking a dogma, a restful solution for their lazy spirits. And they are not satisfied with this alone. They want to be able to place me in one of the pigeonholes where they keep their spiritual retinue, saying of me: he is a Lutheran, Calvinist, Catholic, atheist, rationalist, mystic, or any other of these labels of whose real meaning they are ignorant but which excuse them from further thinking. I do not wish to be pigeonholed because I, Miguel de Unamuno, like any other man who claims a free conscience, am unique. "There aren't illnesses, but sick people," some doctors say, and I say there aren't opinions, but opinionated people.

In religion there is hardly anything which rationally has a consequence, and since I haven't any I cannot rationally communicate it, because only what is rational is logical and transmissible. I do have in my affections, in my heart, and in my feelings, a strong leaning toward Christianity, without embracing the special dogmas of any Christian creed. All who invoke the name of Christ with love and respect I consider Christians, and the orthodox are odious to me, be they Catholic or Protestant —one is as intransigent as the other—who deny Christianity to those who do not interpret the Gospel as they do. I know a Protestant who refuses to admit that Unitarians are Christians.

I sincerely confess that the supposed rational proofs— the ontological, the cosmological, the ethical, etc., etc.— of the existence of God, do not convince me of anything; that all the reasons that can be given to prove that God exists seem to me to be fallacious and question-begging. On this subject I agree with Kant. And I am sorry that in dealing with it I cannot talk to shoemakers in shoe-making terms.

No one has been able to convince me rationally of the existence of God, but neither of his non-existence; the reasonings of the atheists seem to me even more superficial and futile than those of their opponents. And if I do believe in God, or at least believe that I believe in Him, it is principally because I want God to exist, and next, because He reveals Himself to me through my heart, in the Gospel, through Christ and through history. It is a matter of the heart.

Which means that I am not convinced of it as I am that two and two are four.

If we were dealing with something which did not concern the peace of my conscience and my consolation for having been born, I would pay scant attention to the problem; but since it involves all my inner life and motivates all my actions, I cannot satisfy myself by saying, "I do not know nor can I know." I do not know, and that is certain. Perhaps I can never know, but I *want* to. I want to, and that's enough.

I shall spend my life struggling with the mystery, even without any hope of penetrating it, because this struggle is my hope and my consolation. Yes, my consolation. I have become accustomed to finding hope in desperation itself. Let me not hear the superficial and crack-brained shouting, "Paradox."

I cannot imagine a cultured person without this preoccupation, and I expect very little from the realm of culture—and culture and civilization are not the same — that is, from those who are not interested in the metaphysical aspect of the religious problem, studying only its social or political aspect. I can hope for very little contribution to the spiritual treasure of mankind from those men or those peoples who, because of mental laziness, superficiality, scionism, or whatever it may be, ignore the great eternal problems of the heart. I expect nothing from those who say, "One shouldn't think about that." I expect even less from those who believe in a heaven and a hell like those we believed in as children, and still less from those who declare with a fool's conviction, "This is all nothing but fables and myths; those who die are buried and that's the end of it." I have hope only for those who do not know, but who are not resigned to being ignorant, for those who restlessly struggle to learn the truth and who are more concerned with the struggle than with the victory.

Most of my endeavor has always been to unsettle my neighbors, to rouse their hearts, to afflict them when I can. I said this before in my book, *The Life of Don Quixote and Sancho,* in which is found my fullest confession on this subject. Let them seek as I seek, struggle as I struggle, and between us all we shall extract one particle of the secret from God, and this struggle will at least increase our spiritual stature.

To further this work—religious work—I have found it necessary among peoples such as these Spanish-speaking ones, undermined by laziness and spiritual superficiality, half-asleep in the routine of Catholic or free-thinking, socialistic dogmatism, I have found it necessary to appear at times impudent and indecorous, at others harsh and aggressive, and not rarely paradoxical and nonsensical. In our benighted literature one can scarcely be heard even if he forgets himself, screams and shouts from the depths of his heart. For a time the shout was almost unknown. Writers were afraid to appear ridiculous. It was and is with them as it is with many, who allow themselves to be insulted in mid-street, fearing the ridicule of being seen with their hats on the ground and in the custody of a policeman. Not I; whenever I have felt like shouting, I have shouted. Decorum has never checked me. And this is one of the things for which I have been most blamed by my fellow writers who are so correct and so polite even when they are espousing impropriety and inobedience. The literary anarchists are concerned, above all, about matters of style and syntax. When they raise protesting voices, they do it harmoniously; their discords tend to be harmonious.

Whenever I have felt a pain I have shouted and I have done it publicly. The psalms that appear in my volume of *Poems* are but cries from my heart, in which I have sought to start the grieving chords of others' hearts playing. If they have no such chords or if, having them,

6

they are too rigid to vibrate, my cry will not make them resound, and they will affirm that is not poetry, beginning to examine it acoustically. One can also examine acoustically the cry of a man who suddenly sees his child fall dead, and he who lacks both a heart and children will never go beyond that.

Those psalms in my *Poems,* together with several other compositions which I have included, are my religion, my religion in song rather than in logical terms. And I sing it as best I can, with the voice that God has given me, because I cannot reason it. And if anyone sees more reasoning and logic and method and exegesis than life in my verses, because in them there are no fauns, dryads, satyrs, water-lilies, greenish eyes or any other more or less modernistic affectations, let that be his lot, for neither with violin bow nor hammer am I going to touch his heart.

As from the plague I flee from being classified, hoping that I shall die hearing the spiritually lazy, who occasionally stop to listen to me still asking, "What is that man?" The foolish liberals and progressives will consider me a reactionary and perhaps a mystic, without knowing, of course, what this means, and the foolish reactionaries and conservatives will consider me a kind of spiritual anarchist, and all of them a miserable, scatter-brained publicity-seeker. But nobody should care about what fools think of him, be they conservative or progressive, liberal or reactionary.

Since man is stubborn, however, and hates to learn, and usually returns to his former ways even after being lectured for hours, the busybodies, if they read this, will again ask me, "Fine, but what is your solution?" And to rid myself of them I will tell them if they are seeking solutions to go to the store across the street, because mine sells no such article. My intent has been, is, and will continue to be, that those who read my works shall think and meditate upon fundamental problems, and has never been to hand them completed thoughts. I have always sought to agitate and, even better, to stimulate, rather than to instruct. Neither do I sell bread, nor is it bread, but yeast or ferment.

I have friends, and very good friends too, who advise me to abandon this work and bend my efforts toward producing some objective work, something which, as they say, is definite, with something to it, lasting. They mean something dogmatic. I declare myself incapable of it, and demand my liberty, my holy liberty, even to contradict myself if it becomes necessary. I do not know whether anything that I have done or may do will endure for years, for centuries, after my death, but I do know that if one drops a stone in the shoreless sea the surrounding waves, although diminishing, will go on ceaselessly. To agitate is something, and if, due to this agitation, somebody else follows who does something which endures, my work will be perpetuated in that.

To awaken the sleeping and rouse the loitering is a work of supreme mercy, and to seek the truth in everything and everywhere reveal fraud, foolishness and ineptitude is a work of supreme religious piety.

Now you know, my good Chilean friend, what you must answer anyone who asks you what my religion is. Now then: if he is one of those fools who think that I show ill-will toward people or a country by speaking the truth to some of its unreflecting children, the best thing to do is not to answer him.

Concerning Public Opinion

"Most voters do not read newspapers." A newspaper in Salamanca ended its supplement on a recent session of Congress with this quotation. No one will deny it, but I do not believe that the statement by Mr. Maura, which is a truism in Spain, ended there.

A truism because, in a nation where, according to the last census, forty-nine percent of the adults are illiterate and where two-thirds of those who can read and write hardly ever do, naturally the majority does not read papers. And votes are victories.

If the illiterates were not allowed to vote, the general standard would be raised and a great deal would be gained.

Many people will react violently to this statement but it must be repeated—those who do not read newspapers have no opinion on questions which do not directly involve their own personal interests. They are born and live in Spain but they are not true *citizens*.

This is extremely important in Spain where all political parties fondle the masses and strive to conform their platforms to their wishes. The honorable masses are honorable, but they have no opinions or social conscience, and one neither can nor should count on what they seem to think and believe, because in reality they neither think nor believe anything. It is commonly said that our people, our basic social material, is excellent; but all basic social material needs an animating force, an animating force which does not come from within itself.

In Spain certain things are considered as the opinions and beliefs of the majority which are not so at all, because that majority has no opinion nor does it believe the things it has been taught to repeat in chorus. The number of those who show interest, change their minds, decide for themselves, read papers, attend public gatherings and vote spontaneously, without waiting to be taken to cast their vote blindly, is very small. Much larger is the number of the others: illiterate, semi-illiterate, Boetian, and indifferent voters—indifferent either through spiritual laziness or moronic mentality. And it is only the minority that counts or should count. Considering the opinions that officially they are said to have, we have no right to believe that the masses have any. And, for the most part, the minority, which constitutes the public conscience of the nation, does not agree with the dead doctrines buried in the heads of the majority.

This majority furnishes most of those who vote, who sign petitions, who make up a crowd, and who go in droves like sheep through the fields or through the streets, and who cannot read the newspapers; yet they sign the petitions. But, to form opinions and further the progress of public spirit and thinking, those people are neither more nor less; they simply do not exist.

And so it turns out that we are living another lie, the fallacy that Spain is ruled by public opinion. That is not what really rules. The one who pretends to receive his support from the fictitious opinion of a purely numerical majority—I was about to say animalistic in the best sense of the word—and on it bases his right to arrogantly impose his will—is the true demagogue.

There is an opinion which in hallowed, hypocritical language we call reactionary, ultramontane, clerical, or analogous terms which are equally ambiguous. Whenever a newspaper is established to reflect this opinion, no matter how carefully its articles are written, it is never as successful as the more or less liberal papers. Why? Because it does not represent the opinion of the majority. It will be said that it is the opinion of those who do not read papers, either because they read poorly or because they cannot or do not wish to read. And the answer will be that if they should learn how to read and did so habitually, they would abandon those papers eventually, if they did not do so in the beginning. The sentiment of the country is liberal, label its unconsciousness what you will, and I shall have a lot to say about that.

Public opinion is forged by a minority and appears in the papers whose circulation grows for this reason. That minority is the only group in the nation fitted to plan its political course. Anything else is demagogy, not democracy, and among demagogies the red is no worse than the white, which is supported by the votes of those who do not read anything.

A Boetian neither has an opinion, nor reads newspapers, nor votes—measures are approved by false votes—; and when things get a little hot he runs to the hills. The Boetian instinctively abhors everything above his level, everything which leaves the stream in which his dead thoughts are running. It is this demagogical instinct of spiritual levelling that the servants of stagnant tradition are rousing.

Nothing is easier than to say, "My doctrines, the

sentiment that I represent, are the doctrines and the sentiment of the people. Keep silent, work, pray and suffer." For, as these people have no doctrines or sentiment of their own about anything removed from their daily lives and breadwinning, they do not contradict, and keep on being silent, working, praying, and suffering. But the opinion of the others, the only one that really exists, the one that is expressed and made manifest, can reply and contradict.

Of all the lies that surround us and paralyze us, few are greater than the falsity of our democracy, understood as government by the people. It is domination by the illiterate multitude. In Alava, the most advanced province, one-fifth are illiterate; in Jaén, the most backward, far more than one-half are illiterate; and in all Spain almost one-half are illiterate. That is *illiteratocracy*.

Civilization Is Civism

Now that the general elections for the Spanish legislature are over, the lesson that we who dreamt of a spiritual resurrection have learned is well reflected by our dejection.

American readers, do not think that I am going to talk to you about politics. I dislike the subject and I do not like to entertain outsiders with bits of gossip and trifles about domestic life which, after all, concern them not at all. I try to avoid as much as possible the vice of many Spanish writers and publicists who can speak of nothing except their own affairs, "seen from their own national point of view," which is narrow and inexperienced, and I add this last about their own national point of view because I do believe that one should talk about his own house, elevating it and presenting it in the most universal aspect possible.

Starting off, then, with what happened yesterday in our general elections, I am going to outline the principles which have a general application and present the interesting lessons learned from them.

The Government received an overwhelming majority. It is hardly necessary to add that this is the basic factor of our politics. A Government has never been known to lose an election in Spain. To win one it does not have to exert itself very much or put much pressure on the electoral screws. The natural servility of the populace

14

does it. A candidate for the ministry wins largely because he is already in the ministry, protected by the Government, since, just as more individual favors than laws are expected from a representative, it is very convenient to have a minister who is on good terms with those who are running things. And just as in business one way to obtain credit is to create the impression that one already has it, so it is in politics.

They say that Spain is Catholic. Fine, most of the candidates who say that they are Catholics have to spend vast sums to be elected; they have to buy votes. Which means either that the main body of Catholics comes from the poorest classes or that Catholics do not vote unless they are paid. Apparently in Spain Catholicism is something that is bought and sold.

But what I wish to emphasize is the fact that a great majority of the representatives who support the Government are from rural regions. Cities furnish the opposition, and it is only in cities that any thinking is done in Spain. In general the country is submerged in ignorance, lack of culture, degradation, and avarice.

The grandest, noblest and most civilizing thing about the grandiose *Solidaridad* movement in Catalonia has been the city of Barcelona, acting as the guiding conscience of all Catalonia. It has been the civilization of Barcelona, using the term in its strictest sense, that of making a people civil, civic-minded, filled with the spirit of the city.

The city against the country—that is the struggle. Spanish cities are beginning to live in the modern age; the country still lives in the Middle Ages.

Here in the city of Salamanca, in which I am writing, yesterday, on election day, we witnessed a comforting, noble spectacle. A liberal, albeit a lukewarm and timorous one, but a liberal nevertheless, was opposing a fanatical little fellow who was running as a Catholic. The latter, who is moderately rich, was buying votes and was expecting to buy his election. And here in this city, which is liberal, and even somewhat radical as regards the lower classes, the liberal received a resounding majority over the buyer of consciences. Workers with scarcely enough to eat refused the shameful offer.

But the city alone does not comprise the entire electoral district; included are about fifty surrounding villages. And in them the tenant farmers and servants who ceded to their masters' demands and the wretches who sold their votes overcame the liberal candidate's majority in the city. One can find a city worker who, even though he is going to be hungry at night, will refuse the quarter or two offered for his vote, but it is difficult to find a petty village magnate who will not sell himself for a few quarters. It is only a question of fixing the price. Our rustics—perhaps all rustics, at least in Europe,—are characteristically sordid. The villager is greedy and avaricious.

The villager is sadly unconscious. Large groups of rustics do not know who is governing them. They believe neither in law nor in its effectiveness. They are convinced that everything is obtained through pull. It is painful to travel in our country districts, far from the main rail lines and even near them, too. They are asleep in social unconsciousness.

And this unconsciousness is praised; they say that this shapeless mass is the best part of the nation; they exalt the virtues of those vegetative nonentities who give few signs of being alive except bursts of savage primitive passion. The most brutal, the most bestial crimes that I have heard of since coming to this region—one of the most lawless in Spain—have been committed in the country by peasants, not in the city by city dwellers.

We are taught by experience that here the ratio of repugnant, bestial criminality is in inverse proportion to the density of population. The denser the population the more moderate it is and its crimes less repugnant and barbarous.

It is quite understandable, because isolation is the worst counsellor. In a large city strong feelings are much more easily distracted. There a man can be frivolous, but it is harder to be barbarous.

The sad state of unconsciousness of the populace scattered throughout the country regions is an ally of all conservatism and of all tyranny. Your dictator, Rosas, drew his strength from it as did our Carlists. And now it forms the bulwark of the most shameful part of our Government.

And what is happening here is happening elsewhere, is happening in Germany. For it is well known that the Socialist representatives in the Reichstag, although a much smaller group than the Catholic Center, represent a much larger number of voters. The number of voters in the country, divided by the number of representatives, shows about 10,000 for each. Almost all the Socialists represent many more, some as many as 40,000, while there is a Bavarian Catholic representative backed by only four or five thousand votes.

And so it is with the strength of Catholicism elsewhere.

A Catholic was telling me one day of the tremendous increase in his coreligionists in the United States, and I replied, "Yes, just as rabbits are increasing in Australia, because the Irish, Polish, Italian, etcetera proletariat, which makes up North American Catholicism, is very prolific; but tell me, how many men of top rank, statesmen, scientists, philosophers and poets, are Catholics there?"

A similar change is taking place here. The country is overwhelming the city; the rural masses are a terrible chain about the feet of the city dwellers. All political and cultural progress becomes mired in the country. Ruralism is destroying us. This can only be cured by industrializing agriculture, introducing machinery into the fields, and encouraging the grouping of country people into cities.

This concentration is spoken of as a great evil, and it seems to me that that is light talk. Concentration is one effect of the industrialization of agriculture.

I speak again of the origin of the word "civilization." Civilization comes from civil and civil from *cives,* citizen, a man of the city. Civilization was born in the cities and is of the cities. Civilization is Athens, Alexandria, Rome, Venice, London, Paris . . . Sarmiento's vision was in this respect, as in so many others, penetrating and farsighted.

And the majority of Spain is yet to be civilized. Carlism, which is but another term for ruralism—even when city dwellers adhere to it—, because the country can have the spirit of the city, just as the city can have the spirit of the country—Carlism, more or less transformed and under other names, is still the principal obstacle to Spanish civilization.

In my Basque land one frequently hears hymns to rural virtues and the purity of village customs. My

18

Basque countryman from the towns seems superior to the one from the hamlets. In the small towns of my Basque land the cases of unmerciful sordidness which abound in the hamlets are not so frequent—cases where parents are left to die from hunger when they are unable to work. And it is curious to note, too, that the Basque separatist movement was born in Bilbao and received more support in the towns than in the country. The rustic, in addition to being sordid and pitiless, is timorous and suspicious.

And to govern one must reckon with this rural inertia, this tremendous dead weight, and this dangerous unconsciousness. All this sends to the Parliament a drove of great proprietors or their servants, of ignorant lordlings, of coarse sportsmen, of hardhearted millionaires and, especially of nobodies who obey anybody's will.

It is true that the cities, in their turn, send a minority of people somewhat more energetic, awake, inquiring, and upsetting, but it has become the fashion to pretend to disdain them as rioters and humbugs. That whole group of representatives that I mentioned above fails to understand the value of pure agitation, and are indignant at anyone who disturbs their digestion or obliges them to be less servile.

And above all this, sealing it and crowning it, is a most insubstantial and meaningless legalistic system, contemporary Spain. Almost all of our political bosses are lawyers—whether or not they have an office—and those without degrees are just as much lawyers.

I term as a legalistic system the manner of treating everything as if it were a lawsuit before a court, or the particular chicanery practiced in court rooms. The lawyers have contributed all their miserable trickeries,

19

all their repugnant legalism. That legalism appears in the saying, "when the law is made, the trap is laid." There is no worse legislator than the one whose spirit was molded applying laws.

And the lawyer feels a secret sympathy for the rustic, just as the rustic does for the lawyer. Rustics are pettifoggers. Rustic mentality rarely goes beyond the legalist stage. Every villager has a lawyer within, just as a lawyer, however much of a city dweller he may be, tends toward being a rustic. Both are incapable of real sincerity and, consequently, of having a true scientific spirit. One pays so that he will be called right even if he is not, and the other gets paid for making another seem right even if he is not.

And it is the same in politics—the system rests upon rusticism and rusticism on the system.

"The bad thing about the Argentine Republic is its vast extent," said Sarmiento. But the Argentine Republic, since it had no agricultural traditions, since its soil was virgin and unowned, since it suffered from no poorly cultivated ancestral estates of vast extent, although it was hindered by its size, was able very quickly to industrialize its agriculture. In fact, the very facts of its population and area made this necessary. With an area six times larger than Spain, and with little more than one fourth of the population, it has developed a metropolis with more than a million inhabitants. No matter how much the evils—some temporary and some only apparent—of this social phenomenon are exaggerated, the fact remains that the city represents civism and that civism represents civilization.

For some time Barcelona has been discussing civic affairs insistently; it is a sentiment that is being forged there. And the fact is that however much one insists on the deficiencies of Barcelona's sociability—and perhaps I am one of those who have emphasized them most, exaggerating them it may be because it pains me that Barcelona is not perfect—however much we exaggerate them, it is probably true that today Barcelona is the model Spanish city and the place where a city is being formed in all the moral extension of this term.

Barcelona is a city, whereas Madrid is but a capital. Today Barcelona furnishes the example of what all Spanish cities ought to do.

The bad feature is that we neither learn nor take warning, and just as we drove the Cubans and Filipinos into separatism, so we are driving the Catalonians into it. Because the true conspirators of separatism must be sought among those blockheads whose mentality, if not rudimentary, is clumsy, and who insist on stating political problems with violent theological dogmatism and establishing absolute principles. And just as the theologian maintains that he who does not look upon God as he does, does not believe in God, not because of the tests that the theologian establishes, but in spite of them, in like manner the theologians of patriotism condemn as unpatriotic anyone who does not understand and feel about the Fatherland just as they do.

And this crisis in patriotism is intimately related to the conflict between civilization and ruralization. The Fatherland is, more than anything else, the city, just as the Fatherland is a means for civilization and not the purpose of it.

From the Correspondence of a Fighter

But what do you propose? Toward what end are all your efforts directed? What result do you seek? And is it you, my dear and faithful friend, that asks me this?

But it's only natural. You imagine that you are struggling for victory, and I am struggling for the sake of the struggle. And as I can already hear you answering me that the struggle is a means and not an end, I hasten to tell you that I never learned and now know even less the difference between ends and means. And if life, which is only a struggle, is an end, as you say and I don't believe, then the struggle itself may very well be one.

Don't preach peace to me because I fear it. Peace is submission and falsehood. You know my watchword: truth before peace. I put truth in war before falsehood in peace. Nothing sadder than to insist on living in illusions while we are aware of their true nature. When you hear someone say, "We must guard our illusions," consider him hopeless. How can he guard them, knowing that they are illusory? No, my friend, art cannot replace religion.

I seek religion and faith in war. If we conquer, what will be the reward of victory? Forget it; seek the struggle and if you win the victory you will be twice paid. And perhaps the struggle will be reward enough.

Don't you know, perchance, the hours of intimate solitude, when one clings to a resigned despair? Don't you know those hours when one feels alone, entirely alone, when one knows that all that surrounds him is but apparent and fantastical, and when this unreality envelops him and squeezes him like an enormous lake of ice crushing one's heart?

Struggle is clashing and noise, bless them, and that clashing and noise drown out the ceaseless noise of the eternal waters, deep and profound—those that underlie everything, endlessly repeating that all is nothing. These are the waters that are heard in the silence of peace, making it fearful. Struggle is tangible, it is the curling sea lashed by the gale sending its waves to die on the beach; peace is eternity, it is the infinite sheet of the eternal waters. And eternity, doesn't it terrify you? What are you going to do in all of it, poor wave of the sea of souls?

Do you remember those winter nights when around a blazing fire we used to discuss—hopeless consolation—the eternal themes of mortal men. Because there we were men. We were no longer farmers, doctors, and lawyers; each was stripped of his profession and we were men.

The sight of the flames of a fire is like that of the breaking of the sea; the tongues of fire speak to us like those of the waters. Both form only to separate, reform and unite again. And our conversation was that of men in the presence of eternity, of how time is passing, of how they are growing old, of

How death comes softly stealing on,
How soon this life is past and gone,
How silently!

A sublime commonplace and an eternal living paradox! An eternal paradox, indeed, when to be is ceasing to be, when to live is to be dying. And dying, tell me, isn't that perhaps to go on living?

A frightful thing has been happening to me for some time. My heart has turned into an hour glass and I spend my days and nights turning it over. Never has the speed with which time passes been more apparent to me; everything is fleeing from our hands. I knew it, of course. Who doesn't know it? I knew it but I never sensed it as I do now. Not because my past seems greater nor my memories increase, but because my future seems shorter and my hopes lessen. Not because my infancy and with it my obscure birth are fleeting, but because old age is nearing and with it my obscure death. Now do you understand what I mean by "struggle?"

Who believes in the happiness of the old warrior who, surfeited with fighting and no longer capable of it, returns to his home to enjoy his glorious memories? I don't believe in it. Poor veteran! Poor veteran, who consoles his rest with memories of toil!

Rest, yes, when one can do no more. Perchance are you familiar with that gloomy farewell, "Requiescat in pace?" He who rests says farewell.

There are, nevertheless, two kinds of rest: a temporary one in order to return to the struggle after having regained strength, and this rest is like sleep, a preparation for living; and another, definitive and lasting, which is like death, the end of life. And have you never trembled on going to bed with the thought that you may never awaken? Have you not been robbed of sleep by the thought that your sleep might become eternal?

When clever Ulysses went down to the dwelling place of the dead, where the forms of vanquished mortals wander, he met the shade of arrogant Achilles. He tried to console the warrior and the latter responded with these winged words: "There is no consolation for death, illustrious Ulysses; I would rather be a poor farmer's helper on earth than reign over all the dead." In the dwelling of eternal rest Achilles longed for the combats of Troy. Oh, if the sacred city had never been taken! . . .

Again, why do you think Lazarus died the second time, when he died forever? He died of solitude. That man, who had once experienced death and its repose, felt terribly alone among the living who had never died. The aura of eternal rest was in his eyes, in the tone of his voice, and in the rhythm of his step, and his fellow humans trembled before him as before an unknown god. And he felt terribly alone. The reality of the others was not reality for him. Reality! Have you never noticed with what self assurance those who struggle for the momentary victory speak of the meaning of reality? The meaning of reality! This is one of the favorite expressions of those who label everything they don't know—an endless amount—as paradoxical. They think they live in reality because they live on the surface of things, and what they call the meaning of reality is nothing but their fear of real truth. And then they are surprised by the earthquakes which come from far beneath their reality, which is only superficial.

When you have one of those hours in which your soul becomes master of itself and senses its own divinity, remember Lazarus, remember the solitude of Lazarus.

No divine man can have in life the influence that he has after death. No matter how great the work of one who is living, it cannot stir your heart like the work of one who is dead. A dead man speaks. You aren't going to ask him the meaning of reality; that is, to join your party.

Poor Lazarus! The love of his sisters made him live on earth as an exile. He became resigned to this second life and he became resigned to it through his love for Jesus, who shed tears for him. The tears of Jesus, the dew of eternity, were the baptism of his second life. And for Jesus he bore the cross of solitude.

The cross of solitude! Have you never felt on one of those unfathomable nights so quiet, moonless and cloudless, the weight of the stars on your heart? Have you never felt the celestial Milky Way weighing on your soul like a cross of solitude? This usually happens after a day when the struggle grew more intense.

I, when I have felt on my heart the weight of the cross of solitude on one of those unfathomable nights so quiet, motionless and cloudless, have remembered that God gave the world over to the disputes of men and that the kingdom of Jesus isn't of this world.

"Will they understand me?"—you were asking me once; do you remember? And I answered you: "What does it matter that men refuse to understand you, if your words remain forever in solitude?"

Have you not noticed that one of the most frequent watchwords of fathomless human vanity is the phrase, "We do not agree?" The poor wretches can't think of anything to affirm their personalities except, "We do not agree." What does it matter whether they agree with us or not? It is a password; they fear lest their inner selves be caught off guard and stormed.

I don't care, then, whether you agree with me or not, nor whether the others do, since I do not seek them to help me win the victory. I seek them in order to struggle, not to conquer, and I struggle to bear the cross of solitude, for in peace it crushes my heart. I want us all to struggle, for out of the struggle rises love. Fighting with one another men learn to love, to have compassion. Those who lie dead on the battlefield rest together and share a common peace. War has been and is the mother of compassion, which we call love; peace is the mother of envy. Life and calm must be exposed continually; only thus do they attain their just value.

And now, my dear and faithful friend, will you again ask me what purpose lies in all that I do, toward what end my efforts are directed, and what result I seek? Yes, you will ask me again, I am sure. My reply cannot satisfy you, it lacks what you call the meaning of reality, and after reading it you will hear yourself saying, "He doesn't say everything, that is, he really says nothing; there is still something underneath which is left unsaid." No, that which you think I am leaving unsaid is not underneath but above what I am saying to you. You live among the others—you already know who the others are, those that Plato called "the many"—, and those others, whenever they see that someone is not following their road, say, "Bah! Publicity seeker!"

But, after all, what are we going to do? To live is to begin again each day; that is, each day to go on dying. God gave the world over to the disputes of men! Poor world, poor men!

"This letter never was answered," the one who had received it told me when he showed it to me.

Writers and the People

Not long ago Baldomero Argente, a cultured, intelligent and very stimulating publicist, published an article in the Madrilenian weekly *Nuevo Mundo,* bearing the same title that I have used above. His article was reprinted in Mexico, in *El Progreso Latino,* with a note wherein it was stated that it was as pertinent there as in Spain. And since that article is replete with doctrines which I consider injurious both to the progress and splendour of literature and to the general culture of the people, I am going to examine it.

Argente begins by supposing that while he is comparing Spain with Boetia, deploring that the writer, the journalist, the littérateur, and the poet exercise such scant influence on the populace, he is interrupted by the remarks of his interlocutor. He proves his case, and adds that the intellectual influence that the Spanish writer has on his age is almost nonexistent.

"The finest pens," he says, "combat a prejudice or an error in vain; their voices are lost in the desert, and regardless of the efficacy of their arguments, no matter how worthy they may be, their words and their opinion have little meaning; they are denied the faith that our people place so confidently in any quackery, revealing the share of attention given to any spiritual activity in any age. This depression in the influence of writers occasions the seclusion of some, the rebellion of others and the humiliating servitude of the majority, subjected to the self-interested protection, bordering on slavery, of the schemers and pirates of public life who are notably inferior in intelligence and virtue."

This picture does not seem entirely exact to me. I do not believe that the influence of the Spanish writer on his people is less than that of other writers on other peoples, and if we who write frequently complain that we are being neglected, it is because our influence on the public is not reflected in immediate economic gain. Speaking plainly, we are not complaining that not enough attention is paid us, but that our books are not bought. It is quite possible for a writer to have a great deal of influence—at least on certain minds—though selling few books, and for another selling many to have little influence. For, if spiritual influence were to be measured with this yard-stick, it is easily possible that we would discover that the book that has had most influence in Spain is the one that relates the adventures of Bertoldo, Bertoldino and Cacaseno.

Argente's supposed questioner, that is, Argente himself, next deals with the causes of the phenomenon, and he gravely admonishes the writers to place the blame on the backwardness of the public.

"The writers who rebuke a state of society," he says, "because it scarcely heeds them, because it neither follows them, nor discusses them, nor exalts them, forcing them to turn to accommodating rostrums to discuss, with extravagant expectations, the propaganda of their future works, without other audience than their fellows—these are the authors who have never stopped even briefly to examine their own conscience to see if in them may not lie the cause of the evil they deplore."

The self-examination follows next, in which Argente tells us that, "the writers do not write for the multitude, and the multitude fails to find in the writers the voice of its sorrows and of its longings, the song of its sufferings and the beacon for its journey toward an ideal world without sin or suffering."

How nice! And, nevertheless, basically how false! Because, in the first place, every writer who esteems himself and is conscious of the gravity of his profession does well not to write for the multitude, and he does well not to do it for the advantage and benefit of the multitude itself. The multitude does not know its own sorrows or longings; ordinarily the multitude does not know what it wants most or even where to place the blame for its evil. Because if its head aches, it is considered the cause of all ailments.

Then Argente says that it is unnecessary to separate oneself from the crowd, because therein are strength and passion. Neither strength nor passion are in the crowd, nor is there anything more fragile or temporary than the so-called popular writers.

Next he speaks of the ivory tower. Abandoned as it is today, the ivory tower seems more like a prison than anything else; we must go down to the public square and fight for the people, but in fighting for it we do not have to mingle with it and become lost in its ranks or add our voices to the inarticulate cry of the multitude. One can and one should fight for the people, for their good, opposing them if necessary. Even at the risk of spending most of one's life alone and isolated, for many times it is only a day of isolation and disdain that is followed by an evening of respect and glory.

Some lives are a lesson in themselves. Among these is Ibsen's, who after years of absence from Norway, his native land, returned to reap at last the fruits of his rough, unpolished sincerity. Another is Carducci's, whose unconquerable spirit and burning patriotism forced him to call the Italian people, his people, vile.

In a discourse which the great patriot read in August, 1873, before a meeting of the League for the Education of the People, he said, dealing with so-called popular literature:

"Another sign of our old age is the way we always keep separating one type of literature from all others, popular literature. In its virility all literature is popular inherently and necessarily, and in its youth is created more or less by the people themselves. When, in the course of an age that is peaceful and unchanging, a literary school is born which seeks and finds its sole *raison d' être* in the need to proclaim loudly its popular aims and to join the parade of popular forms, and believes that it can and should produce novels, poems and books suited to the people both in style and spirit; when this occurs you can be sure that that age, however many virtues and achievements it may possess in other respects, has an art far removed from its youth and virility. Such a literature, itself old, looks upon the people as a big baby, tells it stories and sings it lullabies. Of course it does not want to appear old and, accordingly, resorts to cosmetics; but in its sweaty effort to apply them, it dissolves their coloring, which seeps away in the wrinkles of the diction; and, falsely garbed as real creative power, suddenly, while affectedly seeking to make its sentimental aims seem useful and moral, the calculating old lady stands forth."

Continuing, Carducci stated that the rising of the masses is a historic necessity but that they should not, even if they wish it, control, or even less, violently destroy, the established order. "They, the youthful current of life, penetrating the other social elements, will disinherit them and, mingling, will become a part of them. Then the state, religion, philosophy and art will wisely and truly be integrated; then at last the people will exist; the people, one, equal, and free."

But, meanwhile, I add, the easiest thing for those writers who seek to go down to the masses, instead of waiting for them to come up to them, is to keep on confusing them and lengthening the holy task of converting the masses into a people, a work already in motion.

One must separate himself from the crowd, and one must do it for the sake and benefit of the crowd itself. When one reaches a peak, whatever it may be, he should open his arms and shout, calling the rest to the peak, rather than descend with the pretext of showing them the way, because he will lose the way himself and he cannot rouse their spirits as he can from above.

It is incorrect to say that the people do not understand, and especially that they do not sense those writers who seem above them; they sense them very well, even though only partially. And here I wish to convey to the reader what I wrote concerning this theme in my book, *Vida de Don Quijote y Sancho,* on commenting on the knight's speech to the goatherds. Without understanding him completely they understand, or better, they sense him very well.

Carducci said that the smiths of a popular literature look upon the people as a big baby. And that is right. And those who write for the people demonstrate puerility, acting like those parents who think that they will be better understood by their babbling children if they babble themselves.

I know of few things that are more deplorable than popular lectures. When a man possessed of certain culture struggles to become popular, he really becomes ridiculous, trivial and vulgar. And more than once I have heard keen workers say on leaving such occasions, "What does he think we are, anyhow?"

To break away from a cold, sterile literature without passion or soul, as Argente says, is one thing, but to join the common crowd is another, and quite different.

Argente adds, "From time to time we hear a bitter discordant note, the explosion of a noble spirit that breaks forth in invectives against the general submission and stupidity. But, excepting those isolated shouts of anger and rebellion, Spanish letters confine themselves almost exclusively to cultivating their garden of egoism."

Carducci's noble spirit hurled bitter discordant notes against the general stupidity; but the deepest, the most profoundly popular Italian poet never lowered himself to mingle with the crowd. He burst forth in the beginning of his *Odas Barbaras* against the fashionable poetry that intrigues the crowd and unhesitatingly sleeps in its embrace.

Perhaps what Argente says about egoism is true. No

less true is what he adds, saying that the writers can redeem themselves if they will remember that to be strongest, not intelligence, not culture, but spirit is most needed. But is spirit, by chance, more easily obtainable than intelligence or culture?

And he concludes, "When the multitude's every affliction is mirrored by a writer, and every obscure presentiment of the social nuclei finds expression in the written word; when writers live not for themselves or their own gain, but make of their souls a constant living offering to their race and their time, then will their race and their time return to them energy, influence, and control over their collective sentiments, and passing through their veins writers will feel the burning spirit which strengthens and rejuvenates—the spirit of good and of truth, without which every literary work is corruptive."

Doubtless this is all very well, but it must be noted that the masses neither understand their afflictions nor recognize at once the one who best portrays them. And it happens all too frequently that they pay more attention to the quack than to the intelligent doctor who understands their ills.

Under the surface of Argente's article, in other respects very well intentioned and in part quite correct, lies the democratic fallacy, that fallacy which is so pernicious for the very people for whose sake it is spread.

A writer has said, "The people hate the truth." And they certainly do hate it when it doesn't please them. The people want to be praised, amused, and deceived, although sooner or later they may end by scorning and rebuffing their flatterers, entertainers, and deceivers. It is necessary, I repeat and shall repeat a thousand times, to struggle for them against their wishes. I understand very well — Why shouldn't I? — why certain writers receive their greatest pleasure from the antipathies they gather around their heads; I understand perfectly — Why shouldn't I?—why they take as the indication of a noble future, not the disdain or the reproach, but the mockery that surrounds them. I sympathize particularly with those lonely spirits that flee from the crowd just when the crowd is about to crown them kings, as Christ did.

Politics and Culture

Of all the Catalonian publicists Luis de Zulueta—a Catalonian who almost always writes in Castilian—is today the calmest, the most comprehensive and endowed with the broadest viewpoint. One seldom finds nobler work anywhere than his in *La Publicidad* of Barcelona.

Now, when political affairs are at white heat in Barcelona and almost every item is dealing with the *Solidaridad*, Catalonian regionalism, etc., we must admire greatly this man who publishes, now and then, in the midst of the noise and dust of the struggle, a few words about eternal questions.

In *La Publicidad* of July 9, the day before yesterday, he has an article entitled *La Educacion Moral* preceded by some observations well worthy of comment.

He begins, "One of the reasons, perhaps the greatest one, for being hopeful amid the present activity, or better, restlessness, in Catalonia is the fact that the present political movement is preceded and accompanied by a ferment of general ideas and an awakening interest in culture.

Liberty, the eternal human ideal, has attempted to take shape in the world, in historical reality, in the most varied forms, from mysticism to political economy. Liberty seems to find expression at present in culture."

Here I must state that it seems to me that Zulueta is deceived by his good will and patriotism. At most the ideas prevalent in Catalonia today are but pretexts to justify their social passions somewhat. Only a few days ago one of the leaders of the Catalonian separatist movement declared that until the problem which is the chief concern of the Catalonians at present is solved, there will be no consideration of the others: all fundamental, permanent, and universal problems of liberty, conscience, and the distribution of wealth, etc.

And there is a great deal to be said about the interest in culture. For in the widely publicized pretence of culture that has been discussed in Barcelona, almost all attention has been focused upon replacing Castilian by Catalan in the schools, more because of aversion toward Castilian than through love for Catalan.

Zulueta continues, "Nevertheless, in culture, in philosophical speculation, in historical investigation, in scientific procedure, Catalonia is still, unfortunately, behind the main current of thought and study. Why should we not loyally admit it? We cannot even match the dozen select scholars who in Madrid, as trustees of the Spanish intellectual tradition, are heroically collaborating in the universal work of science. We do have, indeed, in Catalonia a confidence in our actions that is excessive at times, and, above all, we have a will to act which is never excessive, for one must desire to always, 'desire to even if it is impossible'."

This is not the first time that a Catalonian has made this confession. And it is not improper to add that the Catalonians who have heroically collaborated in the universal work of science have done it in Castilian. Their own language has always been used for lyrical effusions particularly.

And if in Madrid — and in points in Spain other than Madrid — there are scholars that produce heroic work of permanent culture, it is because they live in an atmosphere uncontaminated by political fever.

When a people becomes politically minded, it seems that all other spiritual activities, especially the most elevated, stop and stagnate. Not long ago a Philippine friend wrote me, "Today one cannot talk about works of literature, art, and science here; the young intellectuals are all engrossed in political questions."

And the Catalonian people has always been, and is today more than ever, very exclusively political. The elections of the *Solidaridad* were a political marvel, but their influence on culture is not apparent.

Not many days ago a Catalonian newspaper, commenting on the indifference of the rest of Spain toward the questions concerning the administrative system in the *Law of Local Administration* which is now being debated, said that the debate must be ruled by a mentality unlike theirs, and he would have been right if he had used "inferior to" instead of "unlike."

The truth is that while the Catalonians agitate, become aroused, and talk — the latter in particular — at meetings or *metingues,* at assemblies, and at apelchs and organize all kinds of public political manifestations, the others are slowly and quietly developing their industries, their agriculture, their business and their public school system, without needing to demand for it any more autonomy than they already have.

All Spain is progressing, and doing it rapidly, let the prophets of misfortune say what they will, but Catalonia is not the region which is, relatively, making the most progress. Without becoming agitated or doing a great deal of talking, without *metingues* or assemblies, agriculture is developing in regions which the Catalonians consider dead because it is not their custom to talk. Concerning this progress in the rest of Spain, beside them and, if they insist, against them, one of the most conspicuous of their present political advisers spoke to them recently. They are beginning to wake up.

It is evident that such things are not noticed by one of those traditional traveling salesmen, who on arriving at a town say that it is backward and priest-ridden because it does not have many lofty chimneys vomiting smoke. For many people smoke is still the main indication of progress. But those who can see more than smoke in the sky and more than concrete in the pavement of the streets become informed about such things.

And on the subject of spiritual culture, it is undeniable that for several years people have read much more than formerly, much more attention is paid to public education, and all that talk about the enormous number of illiterates, though it still is repeated, would not be so easy to prove. But, in Barcelona, where public education has always been rather haphazard, it has received no more attention than usual.

Let us return to Zulueta, who, with the next line after the last paragraph that I translated, continues, "These thoughts necessarily arise every time that a book or journal confronts us with one of those themes of experimental psychology, for example, or of religious history, which are the favorite subjects for scientific investigations at present. Any little Swiss or Belgian city makes its contribution to these themes, to a greater or lesser extent, but always much greater than that of a city of 600,-000 inhabitants like Barcelona."

Why is anyone in Barcelona going to study a theme of experimental psychology or religious history? What does this have to do with the political aspirations of their separatist movement? Besides, such themes, although apparently innocent, if they were to become fashionable might introduce the seeds of discord into the party ranks.

Why, this is nothing! Experimental psychology . . . religious history. . . . These things would not be long in dividing us into Liberals and Catholics, and that, before all and above all, is what we want to avoid. For the present, it is most important and most urgent to form a Catalonian state, establish Catalan as the official language, prevent the advances of Castilian, that international language which perhaps is destined to be the most important in the world; afterwards we will deal with the rest, in Catalan.

Ridiculously enough, it has happened that some of the works by those eminent Catalonians who, like Campmamy, Balmes, Pi Margall, Milá y Fontanals, etc., contributed with heroic devotion and in Castilian to the universal work of Science, have been translated into Catalan.

We hope that some day our good friend Zulueta will be convinced that political fever does not furnish the most favorable background for the development of culture. Which does not mean, of course, that a citizen should lose interest in political problems, not even under the pretext that his mind is crowded with problems of science, art, or literature. Nevertheless, Ramon y Cajal did very well when he refused to consider becoming a minister of state. He has another way to serve his country and it, too, has political effects. One of the most pernicious characteristics of our public life is the tendency to enlist the services in politics of anyone who becomes prominent in any field whatsoever of human culture. There are representatives in the Catalonian party who would serve Catalonia better writing sonnets than making speeches.

Hispanic Envy

Once again I am going to refer to the very challenging book *Sick People* by the Bolivian, A. Arguedas. The sick people which Arguedas describes to us is not— I think I have said it before—only the Bolivian people. This people serves as a typical case of an illness that is much more widespread.

In the picture which Arguedas presents of those inland societies, very ingrown, having only infrequent contact with other peoples, provincial and enslaved by routine, one frequently sees the evidence of hate and envy.

"In all those towns and cities," he tells us, "moral and physical life is monotonous and limited. The morality in vogue among them is born, we might say, of uniformity of customs. There is a solid bond among people whose passions are alike and whose intellectual life is identical. That material life without variations or contrasts, always repeating the same things, with clock-like regularity in its social affairs and amusements, finally deadens the imagination and withers the spirit. In the villages an atmosphere of the lowest mentality is formed; everything is subjected to the most careful scrutiny. There is no act which does not come under the collective rule. Private life is an object of general attention; everyone is his neighbor's witness and judge. Gossip and slander are common weapons. In all Bolivian villages, in some more than in others, one notices a tendency to oppress the individual, to make him follow the city style of living. . . ." "In all the villages of Bolivia. . . ." Of Bolivia only? That is a picture of life in almost all provincial societies in which a lofty ideal, certainly not that of making a fortune, has not restrained human nature. The tendency to oppress the individual is a characteristic of conservative, routine societies and of those whose constant, absorbing preoccupation is profit and wealth.

Respect for the individual, which comes from an understanding of the individual, is lacking in such societies. The man who is a man above all is quickly dubbed insane. And if ever he is done justice it is frequently after his death.

Remember Sarmiento. Respected, indeed, but with the respect that a friendly man wins with a ready hand, and, also respectfully, he was called crazy.

The people of those societies, who know each other, have seen really superior men born and brought up but those who have made their fortune are unwilling to recognize the superiority of others. "How can he be talented if he is still poor?" a coarse wealthy fellow was saying recently. And, as soon as one says that someone is intelligent, there are legions who ask, "How much does he make?"

In chapter IV of his work, speaking of the Bolivian national character, Arguedas says that in that society dispersed in widely different communities and with no common ethnic background, the first characteristic one notices is their spirit of intolerance — hate. Ramiro de Maeztu, who wrote the prologue of Arguedas' work, has mentioned in several places that hate is one of the

most noticeable characteristics of our Spanish provincial society. Here nobody can stand anybody; here we
cannot stand ourselves. "That man bores me!", for example, along with a variation of the same that is too vulgar to print, is an expression heard at every turn. Here,
in general, the real man, the true man, the individualist,
is boring. Here just as in Bolivia.

"Everyone who triumphs in any way," says Arguedas,
"engenders in others, not only violent hate, but also, un-
controllable hate, or rather, envy generates hate. A complete absolute leveling is desired. Anyone who rises,
even if only a trifle, above the general standard, instead
of sympathy, meets aggressive irritability."

Envy! This is the terrible plague of our societies;
this is the internal gangrene of the Spanish soul. Was
it not a Spaniard, Quevedo, who wrote that terrible sentence which says that envy is thin because it bites but
does not eat? And this inherited ulcer of ours, twin
sister of warlike idleness, was transmitted to the Span-
ish-American peoples by our ancestors, and it has flour-
ished among them with its offensive bitter flower, perhaps even more than in Spain. Do you not remember
what Lastarria wrote about the action of envy in Chile
even in his day? It is envy, it is Cain's blood, more than
anything else, that has made us easily discontented,
revolutionary and warlike. Cain's blood, envy, that's it.
Was it not a Uruguayan, Reyles, who tried to write in
a novel *La raza de Caín*—a novel filled with intense
mournful pages—the terrible poem of envy?

Collectively we are envious people; we, the Spaniards
on this side of the Atlantic and you, on the other side.

"Malicious, suspicious, doubting, egoistic, and stubborn," says Arguedas, "we live in open combat, without allowing anyone, except the successful politician, to rise above us, and as for anyone who comes here who has not descended to the larval level of our base passions, he is left alone on the heights where, if he feels anything, it is the infinite sadness of one who has nobody to. . . ."

And this dismal cancerous envy has engendered, as a reaction, another illness, the mania of persecution, the sickness of one who thinks he is a victim. Just as when one is apprehensive because of something wrong with him, so when you see that in a country there are many who think they are victims of a conspiracy of silence or of some other vexation, you can be sure that envy is prevalent, even though not one of the complainers has a right to complain.

Only too well do I know that the majority of those misunderstood temperaments who believe themselves the victims of the hostile mediocrity that surrounds them or of the machinations of their rivals are themselves but poor fools; nevertheless, that persecution complex results from a real social condition of actual persecution.

If I were to publish all the letters that I have received from aspiring poetasters who think they are the goal of their neighbors' envy! And if I were to publish those from the others rejoicing at some dig or other that I gave to one of their competitors!

This dilemma of *o bombo o palo,* that is, either adulation or insults, which I have pointed out as characteristic of our criticism, is even more noticeable in America. With nonsensical praise on the one hand and even more nonsensical scorn on the other, one does not know where

to turn. And both are the result of envy, of envy and
a lack of understanding .

Speaking of the Bolivian *mestizo,* Arguedas says that
"to admire he must be educated and to be enthusiastic he
must understand." Is this, by chance, peculiar to him?
We usually pass, both of us, from a lack of admiration
to noisy and indiscriminate admiration. He who admires unreservedly does not admire.

I have two letters from a certain Venezuelan fellow.
In one he flatters me shamefully, in a way that would
make anyone less accustomed than I to such deceitful
praises blush terribly, and in the other he insults me saying "Spanish after all! And poor as the poorest! Here
only the squirrels eat acorns." Between the two letters
he had read two lines of mine about one of his books.
And he was not complaining about my judgment, which
was hardly unfavorable, but about its brevity.

How that hate and envy which Arguedas has noted in
Bolivia and which each of us can observe in this country, spiritually brothers, disguise themselves! "Affection is feigned," says the Bolivian author; "underneath
our honeyed courteous phrases always lie envy, indifference and hate. Our everyday language is filled with
friendly terms, but in use they are trite and meaningless.
There nobody sincerely admires anybody. Fear, respect,
self-interest and hypocrisy cause us to use that flattering language. We must show great affection; inwardly
we are hopelessly incapable of affection. Generosity, nobility, and sincerity are vague terms without concrete
use. They may denote high moral concepts but they show
no friendliness."

Note again the simplicity of those terrible words bearing the awful melancholy of naked truth. Bluntly we are faced with a truth born of sad experience. "Affection is feigned," is completely perfidious and feline. Behind every honeyed courteous phrase envy is always at work. There is more to it than that: envy is very clever at inventing flattery and adulation. Have you not often heard the ambiguous praise of its flattering voice?

One of envy's malicious tricks is to praise indiscriminately the chaff with the wheat, leveling all. Peoples, undermined by envy, are suspicious even of praise. When I hear some one praising some one else excessively I usually ask: "Against whom is that praise directed?" Perhaps against the one who is praised; perhaps against a third party.

Whence comes this horrible gangrenous envy? I believe from spiritual idleness, and remember that a man who is very active making a living, and even a so-called scholar, may have his spirit and intelligence idle. In fact, erudite people are usually envious, keeping their intellects in poorly disguised idleness.

"What I like most about you," I once said to a very worthy man whose spiritual life was most intense, "is that in you I have never observed the least trace of envy." And he answered, "I have never had time to be envious; I am so preoccupied about the road under my feet, and so deeply concerned about whither it will lead me, I have never yet been able to glance at the roads of other people, nor notice who was advancing faster in his own."

Envy is the child of mental superficiality and of the lack of deep personal preoccupations.

Envy springs up among those peoples in whom the

true, intimate, religious urge, creative faith and not para-
sitical dogma, rusts in disuse. Envy, child of spiritual
laziness, is the companion of dogmatism. Not by chance
has the *odium theologicum* become proverbial. And
who knows if envy, rather than gluttony, rather than any
other of the seven cardinal sins, is not the clerical sin par
excellence? Envy infests the religious orders. And it
comes from spiritual idleness.

Peace and democracy almost necessarily engender envy. War is its best remedy. But note well that the
war that accomplishes is the war that one plans against
himself, the war against the mystery of our lives and
of our destiny.

And as for what it does to democracy, I ask if there
has ever been a more envious city than Athens, where
ostracism was invented? The Greek gods envy happy
mortals. It is difficult to express in another tongue the
complete meaning of the Greek word *phthonos,* envy.

Democracies are envious, and because they are envious, at times they have decreed the abolition of honorary
titles, distinctions and medals. And they are very proud
of it. Where there are neither counts nor marquises,
there are generals and doctors. "Like Chinese mandar-
ins," says Argeudas of the rulers of his country, "they
place a great deal of importance upon pomp and show.
. . . Melgarejo wore a red cape; Santa Cruz was covered
with medals, used to begin his decrees thus: Andrés
Santa Cruz, chief citizen, restorer and president of Bolivia, captain general of its armies, general of the Colombian, brigade, grand marshal, etc., etc. A minor but very
indicative point is that this spiritual state is reflected by
every new office holder's desire, be he high or low, to be

photographed with all the insignias of his position: the president, with his tri-colored ribbon and his general's uniform; the ministers, with their tasseled batons; the prefects, with their plumed hats; the plenipotentiaries, chargés d'affairs, attachés, etc., etc., with their embroidered dress coats; the minister, with his plume; the generals, with their sabres drawn; the representatives, with tail coats and white gloves, and so on ad infinitum."

And these expressions of blatant vanity and of luxury itself, that luxury which bursts forth in spiritually idle societies—consider that luxury. Is it not intimately wedded to envy? The other day a very thoughtful, intelligent, and reflective young Chilean, was talking to me about the inordinate luxury of Santiago, and he was telling me that not even in Paris, which he had just visited, in the famous theatres, had he seen luxury equal to that of the ladies of the Chilean oligarchy. And I remember that the unfortunate Luis Ross, that man whose heart was as great and strong as his head, used to speak with me about that same luxury. I remember, too, that once, while telling me about the earthquake in Valparaiso, he said that he might even consider it fortunate if it should happen that it would put an end to the excessive pomp and ostentation. And then, hearing Ross say that, and having recently heard his brother-in-law describe the same scandalous luxury in Chile, I recalled Lastarria's statements which I have already mentioned. And I attributed both plagues, envy and luxury, to the spiritual laziness of a people whose beliefs are either confused or nonexistent, and whose supreme aspiration is wealth and social prominence.

Let me say it loudly and clearly; snobbishness is snobbishness no matter how refined and embellished. He is no less a snob though dressed in the latest Parisian fashion, provided that this is his main concern. Among certain peoples there are social classes for whom luxury —of a certain type—is a painful necessity, a form of slavery, as it is for a bishop to have to dress himself in his pontifical robes on certain days, or for a certain general to have to put on his dress uniform. The performance of this obligation can come to be for them a demonstration of humility. There are obligations and functions which demand a certain amount of pomp and its acceptance may denote a certain amount of modesty. But there is a type of luxury, however refined it may be, however closely it may observe the rules of "good taste," there is a type of luxury which is nothing but snobbishness. It is evidenced in various regions of Spain by country girls whose savings are all turned into fancy earrings, necklaces, bracelets, and jewelry; they are parading their dowry. It is as if they were wearing a price tag.

It is repugnant to me to speak further of this.

Ibsen and Kierkegaard

I can hardly think of Ibsen without recalling a name almost unknown among Spaniards, the name of the human spirit which most deeply influenced his, Soeren Kierkegaard, whose sorrowful soul left its burning imprint on the spiritual life of every Danish and Norwegian youth around the middle of the past century. It was the Ibsenian critic, Brandes, who introduced me to Kierkegaard, and if I began the study of Danish translating Ibsen's *Brand*, it has been the works of Kierkegaard, his spiritual father, that have made me especially glad to have learned it.

Proudhon said that basically every problem is a theological problem, meaning, doubtlessly, religious; a thing that we can be sure of is that underlying Ibsen's drama is the theology of Kierkegaard whose heart, as energetic as it was melancholy, filled with resigned despair during his entire lifetime, fought with the mystery, with the angel of God, as of old Jacob had fought with it, and went to its last resting place after having stamped the truth in letters of fire across the cold dry forehead of his country's official church.

In the last analysis Ibsen's drama is more religious than ethical or aesthetic, and it is not easily understood in its full meaning by those who have not passed beyond the aesthetic and, at most, the ethical conception. And it is because we do not understand it that we call religion a mixture of mythological superstitions and politics.

"Christendom is only playing at Christianity," Kierkegaard shouted, and against everything and everyone he maintained his savage love of truth, of the truth that is felt and not logically conceived, of the truth that is life—he, that noble hermit among men. *Brand,* Ibsen's *Brand* is his reflection in dramatic art, and as long as *Brand* endures Kierkegaard will endure.

I do not understand how anyone can appreciate the real message of Ibsen's work without suffering the spiritual torments endured by that lonely theologian of Copenhagen, and passed on to the equally afflicted and mournful soul of Ibsen, another victim of the Sphinx's evil eye.

In Ibsen's play Inez reminds Brand of those terrible biblical words which Kierkegaard used to quote: he who sees God, dies.

In Kierkegaard's doctrines in regard to the relationship between the two human sexes, to love and matrimony, as he presented them, particularly in his *Euten, Eller,* and in his *Stadier paa Livets Vei,* is the germ of Ibsen's viewpoint on this relationship in the reality of life. It is useless to say that in a drama there is no religious or philosophical doctrine. Perhaps the author has not expressed one didactically but, if he has not seen the reality which lies behind a philosophy or a religion, he has seen nothing which deserves to be perpetuated.

And in these countries where the sexual relationship is understood and felt in the coarsest manner, whether liturgically or sensually . . . in these unfortunate spiritual lands corroded by the most diseased Protean aestheticism, Ibsenian ethics must necessarily remain an undecipherable mystery. Where the blunders of a D'Annunzio are in vogue and where the height of emancipation from prejudices is so-called free love, Ibsen's force cannot well be understood and, even less, felt.

And the same thing is true in other respects. For sexual love is not the core of Ibsen's drama, and even in those plays where that type of love plays a role, it is not the sole end of the conflict. The making of that love into life's most important occupation has been the result less of sensuality than of the mental and spiritual limitation of the poor peoples which the sun beats down upon. For them the biblical temptation, that of the tree of knowledge with the fruit of which our first forefathers were to become like gods, has changed into temptation of the flesh.

I do not know just how it happens, but my experience has taught me that, at least in these parts, carnal lust stifles the proud spirit. And Ibsen's heroes are proud, Promethean, and chaste like all heroes.

In these parts a secret repugnance is felt toward *Wild Duck;* what we call beauty is but a procuress of cowardice and lying. What we call art is but the green flowering cloak which covers and protects the pool of foul stagnant waters harbouring a consuming fever. The *Pillars of Society* are needed to withstand *An Enemy of the People. Ne quid nimis,* repeat the miserable ones facing the "all or nothing" of Brand.

"Let others complain," said Kierkegaard, "that times are bad; I complain that they are petty because they lack passion. Men's thoughts are as flimsy as thin ice and men themselves as insignificant as the snow that covers it. Their thoughts are too petty to be sinful. A worm might consider such thoughts sinful, but not a man created in the image of God. Their pleasures are circumspect and boring; their passions, sleep; these materialistic souls fulfill their duties, but, like Jews, they collect their usury; they believe that although our Lord keeps his accounts in good order, they can hand him counterfeit. Out with them! This is why my soul always hearkens back to Shakespeare and the Old Testament. There one feels that those who speak are men; there they hate; there they love; there they kill the enemy, curse their descendants for generations to come; there they sin."

Having read this, do you not understand the heroic morality of Ibsen's drama?

And I do not speak of anarchy, for this has come to be, among us, by dint of nonsensical acts and brutal stupidities, a word without clear meaning.

Now tell me, do you think that all those proficient youngsters who are to be statesmen and academicians are capable of sinning? Their aspirations are too petty to be sinful.

And neither should you believe, my youths, that sin is particularly limited to the realm of sexuality. It is not! We cannot call that stupid braggart Don Juan, a complete idiot, an Ibsenian, Shakespearian, or Biblical sinner, and if the ghost of the Knight Commander had not carried him off in time, he would have become a respectable old man, defending the Order, the venerated traditions of our ancestors, the superficial liberty of our day, and the established beliefs, and piously attending the solemn ceremonies of his Brotherhood. His animal intelligence would have checked him at this point.

IBSEN AND KIERKEGAARD

Are we not united here to honor the memory of Ibsen? Well, let us try to awaken within ourselves, now that we are united to honor him, something of the spirit of his spirit, without limiting ourselves to speaking of the author as a mere author, with that pestiferous professional indifference toward the basic religious and ethical meaning of his concepts. To do otherwise is not worthy of us or of him. We must leave that to the repugnant aestheticians.

I am not going to speak of his style, then, or of his technique. I cannot judge his theatrical technique, nor do I care to. Theatrical technique and all that gibberish as to whether or not a thing is dramatizable are on a level with collecting quarterly payments. If one of Ibsen's dramas should please the audience in one of our theatres, I would begin to doubt its worth.

Thanks to God, I have never witnessed the representation of any of Ibsen's dramas; I have not seen one defiled and presented as a show, together with a crowd of men and women who will never die on account of having seen God's face. I have not had to endure, on leaving the theatre, hearing the eternal and unbearable nonsense about whether this or that role is better played or whether this or that scene more probable.

Probability to those ladies and gentlemen means vulgarity. Confronted with the hero's conscience, they ask, "What would I do in such a situation?" And the answer is, "Anything, except what he does." They conclude that he is unnatural. They do not like to see any exceptions because the exceptions affront them. I have never heard the gentleman who has just made his debut in Parliament—another theatre—saying yes or no

55

as Christ teaches him to, after having heard the fiery
words of Brand, for this shepherd of Norwegian souls is
unreal because he, the good mono-syllabist, never found
Brand on canvassing the district, and if he passed near
him, he did not recognize him, for Brand does not produce votes. "The victory of victories," Brand shouts,
"is to lose everything." And this is not understood by
those. . . .

Most people go to the theatre to see and hear what
they see and hear every day dressed up a bit with literary
and aesthetic trimmings, to see themselves in the mirror
of daily reality, and it is for that reason that I do not
go there. The characters portrayed there are the same
ones that continually are embittering and harrassing my
life. Neither in life nor in our theatre do I find either
the tormented heroes or souls of Ibsen. They would be
thrown from the theatre by our honored middle class in
the name of "good taste," that repugnant, nauseating
"good taste." Those good Sadducees do not wish to spoil
their digestion.

Let my commemoration of Ibsen on this occasion be a
protest in his spirit; a protest against the miserable ostentation of good taste and the *Ne quid nimis;* a protest
against the pettiness of these times in Spain, when the
revered name of Ibsen, together with the no less revered
name of Nietzsche, is used to cloak the temerity with
which employment and social standing are bought and
sold.

We are not paying tribute to a littérateur.

Ibsen, the solitary, the strong—"nobody is stronger
than he who is alone," Schiller said and repeated—Ibsen,
the great disdainer—a disdainer like Carducci, another

radiant spirit which has just entered the shades of death —Ibsen was not what we call a littérateur; he certainly was not.

Ibsen forged his spirit on the hard anvil of adversity, far from the brutifying gatherings in literary charity-huts, exiled and alone, and full of faith in himself and in the future, alone and remote from that so-called republic of letters which is but a fair of gypsies and horse traders.

Ibsen did not defame, nor did he have anything to do with the vile bartering of praises or the degrading today-for-me-and-tomorrow-for-you system. On the contrary, he calmly awaited, not his hour, but the hour of his work, the hour of God, without impatience and without despair.

He waited until his compact audience of readers was formed instead of immediately turning to the dissipated public. And so his old age, like that of Carducci, was a solemn sunset in a clear sky over the fjords of his native land crowned by glowing golden clouds.

His life was a dramatic poem of ferocious independence, just as that of Kierkegaard, his master, had been a tragic poem of heroic solitude.

Solitude is the favorite solution in Ibsen's dramas, solitude is the refuge of those proud and robust souls who travel onward cutting through the dead sea of the multitudes who, under the yoke of routine, busy themselves multiplying and growing, satisfying their stupid enslaving flesh.

The Moral Urge

Today I feel like talking of a country which I have never visited, which I know only through books, magazines and newspapers which come to me from there, through letters and reports of people who know it by sight.

I have just read in the *Nuova Antologia* of Rome, in the September sixteenth number, an article by Amy A. Bernardy entitled *Americanismi*. In it we are warned against all the tourists and travellers who go to the United States for the purpose of writing an article on American life. "The German who has spent a month in Milwaukee, the Frenchman who has travelled from New York to San Francisco on the Overland Limited, the Austrian who has spent a month attending the Embassy teas in Washington, the international reporter who has seen the president at a banquet, a prizefight in the slums of New York, the Chicago stockyards, the Indians even though on a reservation, Niagara Falls and the Mormons, says he has seen America." And Madam Bernardy tells us that it is not enough to have seen it, but that one must have lived it, and she warns us against the works by Giacosa, Ugo Oritti, Max O'Rell, Le Roux, Bourget, etc.

As for me, I can state that every time in speaking with an Argentine or a Spaniard who has lived there several years, I express any opinion of that country which I acquired from the sources that I already mentioned, he interrupts me saying, "Oh, no; one must have lived there." Many people have said this to me, and since their respective opinions differ widely, I am convinced that they, in their turn, have only a very limited idea of their own country or of the one where they have lived for a long time. How true is the proverb: "What a man says of the fair, reflects the kind of a time he had there," and equally true—I have proved it a hundred times right here—that the natives of a country do not notice things that seem self-evident to the newcomer. They have no basis for comparison.

All of which has led me to a paradoxical conclusion—since they have started saying that I cultivate the paradox I shall not disappoint those who say this—which is that to write about a country it is best not to visit it but to gather as many reports about it as possible and study them, making very careful comparisons of them all. I am quite confident that if a Greek of the time of Pericles or a Roman of the age of Augustus were to come to life and read what has been written about that Greece or Rome, he would exclaim, "I had to come back to life after all these centuries to know the world I lived in!" The person who lives in a country is so close to the trees he cannot see the forest.

Indirectly, then, I have gone on forming my idea of what Argentina really is, and all the corrections I receive from those who know it by sight serve only to complete, round out and corroborate my idea.

I have two main sources of information: one, cosmopolitan, and the other, native. As soon as I encounter a new informant, whether he is speaking or writing to me, I try to find out which point of view he voices.

Both tendencies are like two pairs of glasses modifying correct sight; one of the shortsighted, the other of the farsighted. And you see just as poorly through one pair as the other.

All speak of the material and economic progress of the Río de la Plata region and of the wealth and splendor of Buenos Aires. From books such as *La nación en marcha* by Mr. Bernardez, we can form a very complete idea of that progress.

In Spain we have a very good book wherein to seek such information, *Sangre nueva: impresiones de un viaje a la América del Sur,* by Mr. D. Federico Rahola, who took a trip there with Mr. Zulueta. Even the most shortsighted person will have no difficulty in understanding it.

It is quite different, however, when we attempt to seek out more intimate details: its spiritual atmosphere, its typical character, its sociability. Practically my only sources of information in this respect are literary works, that is, literature. And literature—I have said and repeated it a thousand times—is only literature. Beginning with gaucho literature, *Martin Fierro, Fausto, Santos Vega,* for instance; not omitting Gutiérrez's novels, and including even the most recent, now more refined and polished, productions of the gaucho genre, my reading has familiarized me with the world which it has painted—a world which has now disappeared and which perhaps never existed just as it is represented to us. Neither have I neglected the historical field. I have devoted hours to reading: General Paz, Sarmiento, López, Estrada, Saldías, Juan Augustín García, and Pelliza, and, finally, I have perused such widely different work as *La Tradición nacional* by Dr. Gonzalez, and

Nuestra América by Dr. Bunge.

In many of these works, and especially in the most recent, it is evident—I have said this before—that their authors, even though Argentines, see Argentina through European eyes. The world that surrounds them, in which they live and from which they receive sustenance, is judged by the sociological doctrines of the *Bibliothéque de philosophie contemporaine,* edited by Alcán in Paris, or from some similar source. I mention Mr. Ingenieros as an extreme example of this.

One should add the influence of opinions like those of Pablo Groussac, for instance, a Frenchman who, true to type, has remained loyal to the spirit of his fatherland in which he lives, always judging Spanish-speaking countries with one spirit, the French spirit, which has never been able to understand them intimately.

Thus it happens that today my best source of information concerning the spirit of those regions is the news stand, and most especially—let no one be surprised— *Caras y Caretas.* It seems to me that the numbers of *Caras y Caretas* mirror the average Argentine spirituality, or rather the lack of it, and particularly that of Buenos Aires, just as the numbers of *Blanco y Negro* reflect the present spiritual poverty in Spain and, above all, in Madrid.

Everyone has his particular interest, and mine is that of the spirituality, of the intimate state of the consciences of a people, of their deepest preoccupations, that is, of their religious situation. Very often when I have asked some one from that region how religion is regarded there, he has answered me, "No one pays any attention to such things there; they are busy enough making money; if anyone looks at the sky it is to see

61

whether or not it is going to rain." Of course I have not believed them because I well know that there are people who hide their intimate preoccupations and I know, also, that, for the majority, religion does not go beyond concrete, dogmatic, ritualistic forms such as a confession in church. On the other hand, others have told me of some remains of priestly influence in isolated regions and of the forms of the cult, of the ladies' gatherings and of all that lamentable comedy which turns Catholicism into something stylish, becoming, and in good taste.

This good taste, high society, and "high life" of the upper classes is one of the worst scourges of those new countries which, though democratically set up, long for an aristocracy.

Perhaps titles and decorations would cure them of that vanity born of superficiality. The title of doctor has been substituted for that of baron or marquis. Snobbishness is undermining their spirits.

Not a copy of *Caras y Caretas* comes without a lengthy description of the wedding of the So-and-sos with a picture of the bride and groom emerging from the nuptial ceremony surrounded by friends and relatives. All of which does not matter one whit to anyone else.

This seems to reveal an insane madness of exhibitionism, a madness like that which led one poor fellow to shoot himself so that his picture would appear afterwards in a stylish weekly. I don't know whether or not it happened just as the magazine reported it, but *si non è vero, è ben trovato,* and says all that can be said. And just as that poor victim of exhibitionist madness killed himself in order to become famous for one week, it is easy to believe that someone might get married only to have his portrait appear beside that of the bride. That morbid madness, which evidences a lack of depth, produces two plagues: that of the interview and that of the postcard. All life seems to be on the surface, to be concerned with appearances. One might say that people spend half of their lives making a fortune and the other half buying vanity with it.

Thus even the dignity of the gravest functions is forgotten. When I saw the autograph of a bishop of the Roman Catholic Church blessing the readers of the weekly and then the picture of the prince of the Church as he blessed them, I said to myself, "Thanks, dear God, because, as yet, in spite of our spiritual lack, we have not reached that point; here no bishop would have anything to do with such a thing." And I recalled the terrible prophetic invectives of the great Portuguese poet Guerra Junquiero in the prose epilogue of his poem *Patria* and I thought that the day will arrive when we see a snapshot of a fashionable priest at the moment when he turns in the celebration of the mass to raise the Host for the adoration of the faithful.

These typical details speak more fluently about the intimate state of our religious or irreligious conscience than whole volumes. They reveal that the inner life, the spiritual life, must languish in a fearful vacuum, especially among women.

Women! They are the real problem in those new countries, made of alluvium, of people from the four corners of the earth, where men's thoughts are almost always limited to business. It is the women who are forging the soul of the United States; the women who are concerned with eternal questions even though surrounded by follies. Everyone who writes about the great American beehive dwells at length on the North American women.

Women are the true principle of continuity in a people, the ark of its most prized and profound traditions. And in a country which is taking shape, in a country which is striving to acquire personality—the only way to enjoy real independence and permanence—, in a country which needs a strong tradition, just as every torrential changeable river needs well rooted trees along its banks; in a country of this type, few things, if any, are more vital than the preoccupations which guide the spirits of its women. And if their main preoccupation, among the moneyed classes, should be the so-called society life in which the church is on a level with the theatre and really but another aspect of it, and if beliefs—you may call most anything that—and worship should form part of the requirements of good taste and education, the country in which this is true would be in very grave danger.

With the information at my disposal I do not dare to discuss this matter in greater detail in connection with this young republic, but on reading certain things I sometimes think that Sarmiento, swayed by his European centered optimism, by the outspoken faith that he placed in the moral influence of the dresscoat and the manners that he called civilized, never foresaw that the day might come when it would be necessary to turn to barbarism—what he termed barbarism—to cure what he called civilization, and died without having suspected perhaps that, had it not been for the spirit of Rosas, the spirit of Rivadavia or that of Sarmiento himself might have ruined his country. Because the noble progressive enthusiasm of the latter two is being converted into mere snobbishness.

I feel I must declare it sincerely and honestly. From among the many literary works which I receive from Argentina and South America in general, I can choose a few which have some merit, some spark, or a certain amenity, or clever imitation of European models, French especially, or some other quality which makes them not always contemptible but even acceptable at times. What they all lack is intensity and austerity of feeling, depth of spirit. Apparently they have never felt the vivifying breath of the great noble preoccupations, the eternal preoccupations of the weary human race.

And without this background of eternal restlessness, always renewed and never satisfied, the restlessness which has produced all the great works of the human spirit, without this background, even exterior civilization, that of commercial and industrial progress, finally languishes. For the one who would like to see this dealt with further, I recommend *Principles of Western Civilization* by Benjamin Kidd.

What ruins Spanish-speaking peoples—I have said it many times and in many ways, and I shall repeat it many more times and in new ways—what ruins them is their materialism disguised as practicalism. There is nothing less practical than that which is ordinarily called practical. Materialism appears among one after another of those peoples, sometimes cloaked with idealism. The forms of religion are really and truly material and so are the forms of irreligion which are derived from them.

Spanish free-thinkers profess freethinking á la Spanish Catholícism; they substitute quasi-scientific superstition for religious superstition—they speak of Reason and Science, both with capitals—, and, if formerly they used to swear by Saint Thomas, now they swear by Haeckel or by any other atheistic exponent of free-thinking.

"If you want to get ahead in this world, don't worry about the next." I have heard this statement a thousand times and I think it is a bit of solemn nonsense. One individual can live very well and can live even a noble spiritual life without being preoccupied about the other life, because the people among whom he lives and on whom he depends, have prepared for him the moral framework for his conduct, just as a parasite lives, with certain exceptions, in the digestive tube of a higher animal—according to the exact metaphor of Mr. Balfour, a former prime minister of England—, since said individual receives, in the form of honor or some other sentiment, moral juices refined throughout centuries of Christianity; but a whole people cannot live today without preoccupying itself about this.

What they say about Japan in this respect seems to be fabulous. Social life would be just as impossible if everyone were convinced that individual consciousness ends at death as it would be if all were convinced absolutely of the existence of a heaven and a hell, like the Catholics. In both cases it is a basic uncertainty that serves as a moral urge.

And, since this question is at once very profound and very elusive, I think it best to interrupt these reflexions at this point, leaving myself free to reopen it at some future date.

Truth And Life

One of those who read *My Religion* has written me asking that I amplify or clarify the statement that I made in it that truth must be sought in life and life in truth. I am granting his request.

First, truth in life.

It has always been my conviction, growing ever deeper with the passing of time, that a man's supreme virtue should be sincerity. The ugliest vice is lying, with its derivations and disguises, hypocrisy and exaggeration. I prefer the cynic to the hypocrite, when it is possible to make a distinction.

I profoundly believe that if we were always to speak the truth in every case, and nothing but the truth, at first the world would threaten to become uninhabitable, but before long we would understand one another as we do not today. If we could all pierce the wall of others' consciences and freely see each others' souls, our grudges and suspicions would all merge into an immense mutual piety. We would see the blemishes of the one we consider a saint, but also the good points of the one we regard as a knave.

And it's not enough not to lie, as the eighth commandment of God's law orders us, but it is also necessary to speak the truth, which is not entirely the same thing. Progress in spiritual life consists of passing from negative to positive precepts. He who neither kills, nor fornicates, nor robs, nor lies, possesses a purely negative uprightness, and is not thereby on the road to sainthood. It is not enough not to kill, one must better and enrich the lives of others; it is not enough not to fornicate, one must evidence the purity of his feelings; it is not enough not to steal, one must contribute to the general good of all; it is not enough not to lie, the truth must be spoken.

I must make a further comment—and hereby I make answer to a malicious unsolicited criticism as well—to the effect that since there are many, many more truths to be said than time and occasions in which to say them, we are not going to allow anyone else to choose those which we shall utter. Whenever anyone tries to persuade us to proclaim certain truths, we can reply that if we did as he would have us do, we would not be able to proclaim others we hold more timely and of greater moment. And not a few times it happens that what he believes to be true and supposes we do likewise, is not the truth at all.

And let me caution my malicious critic that although I do not esteem the poet he is asking me to join him in attacking, neither do I esteem the other that he admires and wrongly supposes that I must admire. Because although one in his uneven style does nothing but dress a lifeless puppet in tawdry ornaments, flounces and braid, at times the other says substantial and courageous things —among many blunders—, but they are almost never poetical, and, above all, he says them in a deplorable fashion, partly because of his insistence on subjecting them to rhyme, which resists him. And I will speak of this at greater length in an article entitled *Neither One nor the Other*.

And turning to my present theme, since I think I have said enough about seeking truth in life, I turn to the other, seeking life in truth.

There are dead truths and living truths, or, better: since truth cannot die or be dead, there are people who receive certain truths as purely theoretical, lifeless things, which do not vivify their spirits at all.

Kierkegaard divided truths into essential and accidental ones, and the modern pragmatists, headed by William James, judge a truth or scientific principle according to its practical consequences. And so, to one who says he believes that there are inhabitants on Saturn, they say, "Which things that you now do would you not do, or which things that you do not do would you do, provided you did not believe this planet to be inhabited, or how would you change your conduct if you changed your mind in this respect?" And if he answers that his conduct would remain unchanged, they reply to him that this is not believing or anything that approaches it.

But this criterion, developed in this way—and I must confess that the leaders of the school do not develop it so abruptly—is unacceptably narrow. The cult of truth for truth's sake is one of the disciplines which most elevates and fortifies the spirit. Among most erudite people, who are usually mean and envious, the continual search for little truth, the struggle to correct a date or a name, is no more than a sport or a monomania or a point of vanity; but in a man with a calm and elevated soul and among the erudite whose erudition might be called religious, such searchings denote a cult of truth. For he who is not accustomed to respect it in little things will never learn to respect it in big ones. And it must be remembered that we do not always know what is big and what is little, or the importance of the possible consequences that can result from something which we consider not only little, but trifling.

We have all heard of the religion of science, which is not—God deliver us!—a grouping of philosophical principles and dogmas derived from scientific conclusions and intended to replace religion, a fantasy caressed by those poor scientific dabblers of whom I have already spoken. It is the religious cult of scientific truth, the submission of one's spirit before objectively demonstrated truth, the humility of heart to surrender to what reason shows to be truth, wherever it may be and even if it does not please us.

This religious feeling of respect for truth is not very old in the world and those who boast of it most do not possess it. During the first centuries of Christianity and the Middle Ages, pious fraud — that's right, *pia fraus* — was current. If anything was considered edifying, that was reason enough to see its acceptance as truth. All that the four Gospels have to say about Mary's husband, Joseph, can be put on a cigarette paper, but some one has written a *Life of Saint Joseph, the Patriarch* of more than 600 pages. What can it contain but speeches or pious frauds?

Occasionally I receive the writings, now of Catholics, now of Protestants—more from the latter whose proselytism is more energetic—in which they are trying to prove this or that according to their credo, and in them one finds very little love of truth. They twist and outrage the texts of the Gospels, interpreting them sophistically and speciously to make them say, not what they say, but what they want them to say. And so it turns out that those exegetes afflicted with rationalism—I am not referring, of course, to the systematic detractors of Christianity, like Nietzsche, or to the superficial spirits who write dissertations trying to prove that Christ did not exist, that he was a disciple of Buddha, or some such phantasmagoria—those exegetes have shown in their religious cult of truth a religiosity far more extreme than that of its systematic detractors and refuters.

And this love and respect for truth and the search for life in it can be employed in seeking truths which seem less pragmatic to us.

In his *Parmenides* Plato had Socrates say that he who does not train himself, when he is young, in analyzing those metaphysical principles which the populace considers idle and the concern of idlers, will never arrive at any worthwhile truth. That is, as they say today, he whose nose is so close to the dollar that he cannot see a joke, will never experience an ennobling thought. His coffers may be filled with gold, but Boetian stupidity will fill his soul. And, centuries later than Plato, Bacon, quite different but also lofty in spirit, could say, "We must not consider useless those sciences which have no use, provided that they train and discipline the mind."

This is a sermon that should be preached daily—and I shall do my part—in those countries where mechanical development is crowding out all competitors.

Amongst the crowd this is inevitable since it judges only by what it sees, feels and hears—mechanical effects. Thus, it is quite natural that seeing the telephone, the phonograph, and other apparatuses which they say Edison invented—although they really only partly belong to this clever technical impresario—they think that Edison is the wisest and greatest living physicist, and they are ignorant of even the names of many others whose science is more profound. They have never seen any apparatus invented by Maxwell so they choose Edison, just as they keep on believing that the fantastic popularizer Flammarion is a stupendous astronomer.

And the latter, with his pseudo-science, will be especially famous in countries like that (Chile), formed mainly of emigrants from all parts of the world who are seeking their fortunes and, once having made them, try to become educated overnight; in countries where noble philosophical studies enjoy no public esteem and where pure science bows to engineering, which fills one's pockets. At least, temporarily.

I say temporarily, because where culture is complex the practical value of pure speculation is recognized and Hegel and Kant share in the military and industrial triumphs of modern Germany. There they know that although when Staudt began the study of pure geometry it was no more than mental gymnastics, today it serves as a basis for a large part of integral calculus which is useful even in the laying of cables.

But, aside from the mediate or indirect usefulness which the scientific principles which seem most abstract can have, is the fact that their investigation and study educates and trains the mind much better than the study of their scientific applications.

As we begin to curse pure science, which we have really never cultivated—that is why we curse it—and speak only of practical studies, without completely understanding what this means, the countries in which scientific applications have been most stressed are beginning to learn by experience and to distrust their "practical" counselors. A mere engineer—that is, an engineer without true scientific spirit, because some do possess it—can be as useful in laying out a railroad as a mere lawyer in defending a suit; but the former will never make a contribution to science and the latter should never be entrusted with the reform of the constitution of a people.

To seek life in truth, then, is to seek, in the cult of truth, to ennoble and elevate our spiritual life and not to convert truth, which is and always must be living, into a dogma, which usually is dead.

Men fought in passion for years over whether the Holy Spirit comes from the Father only or from both the Father and the Son, and it was as a result of this struggle that *Filioque* was added where it says *qui ex Patre Filioque procedit* in the Catholic creed. But what Catholic becomes impassioned about that today? Ask the most pious Catholic and the one with the deepest faith even among priests, why the Holy Spirit must come from the Father and the Son and not only from the Father; ask what difference it would imply in our moral or religious conduct whether we believed one thing or the other, without taking into account the question of submission to the Church which so orders us to believe, and you will see what he answers you. And the fact is that what was once the expression of intense religious feeling which can to a certain extent be called true faith— I do not hereby affirm its objective truth—today is only a lifeless dogma.

And the present Pope's condemnation of the doctrines

of so-called modernism is occasioned only because the modernists—Loisy, LeRoy, P. Tyrrell, Murri and others —are seeking to instill true life into the dead dogmas, and the Pope, or rather his advisers—the poor fellow is incapable of such deep penetration—foresee with great clarity that as soon as one attempts to vivify such dogmas, their ruin is complete. They know that there are corpses which, when touched, dissolve into dust.

This is the main reason why we should seek the life of whole truths so that those that seem to be whole but are not will appear as they really are, as untruths or merely apparent truths. And the exact opposite to seeking truth in life is to forbid any examination and declare that there are intangible principles. There is nothing which should not be examined. Unlucky the country where patriotism cannot be analyzed!

Behold how truth in life and life in truth are interwoven; those who do not dare to seek the life of the truths they profess will never live with truth in life. The believer who refuses to examine the fundamentals of his belief is a man living in insincerity and in falsehood. The man who is unwilling to consider certain eternal problems is a hypocrite and nothing but a hypocrite. And thus, both in individuals and in peoples, superficiality is usually found side by side with insincerity. An irreligious nation, that is, a nation where hardly anyone is interested in religious problems—whatever the accepted solutions—is a nation of hypocrites and exhibitionists, where it is important, not to be, but to seem to be.

And I have put before you what I understand as truth in life and life in truth.

The Spanish Christ

He was a South American, who arrived from Paris. "These Christs, Heavens"—he said to me before one of the goriest paintings that hang in our cathedrals—"these Christs . . . this is repugnant, unnerving!" "To anyone who does not understand something of the cult of suffering," I said to him and he answered, "But suffering and blood are not the same; there is bloodless suffering, there is calm suffering." And we began to talk about it.

I confessed to him that my soul is like that of my nation, that I like those drooping, livid, bloody, wounded Christs; those Christs that have been called savage. Have I no artistic taste? Am I barbarous? I do not know. I also like the gloomy Virgins, disfigured by grief.

"The Spanish Christ," Guerra Junqueiro has often told me, "was born in Tangiers." Perhaps he is an African Christ. Would he be a truer Christ if he were Greek, or Parisian or English? Because there is no possibility of recapturing the historical one, the Galilean. And as for applying history to Christianity . . . it is a question of twenty centuries, and here, in Spain, history is Spanish. He was born, then, perhaps in Tangiers. Saint Augustine was born not very far from Tangiers.

Bloodless, calm, purified suffering . . . yes, stylized or, shall we say, artistic suffering; the cry of anguish that comes from the flageolet as a dirge. Very well. This is the feeling that the Laocoon group inspired in Lessing.

Very well, but this case parallels that of irony. Usually those who do not become indignant are ironical or "ironists"—I prefer to call them "ironists."

He who becomes indignant, becomes insulting. The "ironist" pardons everything and says he does it because he understands everything. Could it be that he doesn't understand anything? I don't know.

"Not everyone," I said to my South American friend, "can stand our harsh rude ways." It has been said that hate abounds in Spain. Perhaps; we begin by hating ourselves. Here there are many, many people who do not like themselves. We follow the precept, "Love your neighbor as yourself," and since, in spite of our inevitable egoism, we do not love ourselves, neither do we love our neighbors. The hermit and the meddler are formed in the same way. And do not think that the hermit cannot be egoistic; he can be very much so. But, even if he is, he cannot love himself.

"When you see a bullfight," I continued, "you will understand these Christs. The poor bull is also a kind of irrational Christ, a propitiatory victim whose blood cleanses us of not a few barbarous sins. And leads us, nevertheless, to new ones. But, does not the pardon lead us, poor humans that we are, to sin anew?"

My friend has seen a bullfight in Madrid and he writes me, "You are right. The Spanish people like harsh spectacles that arouse tragic or, rather, ferocious emotion. It has been confirmed in diverse conversations, especially in those with writers who seem to enjoy ripping each other to pieces with unequalled ferocity. Poor Christ pierced and bathed in blood! I have no hope that his wounds may heal or that his agonized expression may disappear here in these Spanish cathedrals. Here they do not realize that, after his martyrdom, Jesus returned to Heaven."

Who knows? Perhaps our Heaven is martyrdom itself.

The ferocity with which men of letters attack each other here has been noted by more than one stranger who has come to know us. Yes, here all men, but artists and literati in particular, dissect one another with a ferocity that is bull-like, or perhaps Christian, in our African way.

And I, who do not like bulls and who never go to see them; I, who do not like to skin my fellow writers because the trade of butcher dirties one's hands, do like the African Christs, exhausted, bloody, livid and wounded. Yes, I like those bloody drooping Christs.

And as for the taste for tragedy, that above all!

In order to maintain the popular theatre they have had to cram a bit of tragedy into it. Comedy, high comedy, with its irony and other refinements, is eminently suited for the bourgeoisie but hardly at all popular.

When I was a student about 1880, I used to go to the theatre—and I thought I was in paradise—where the common people went. And I mingled with them and was one of them. How *Don Alvaro, or the Power of Fate* penetrated to the very marrow of the bones of those honest masons, tailors, carpenters and butchers!

One should read the comparison that the great Sarmiento made, after his trip to Spain in the middle of the

last century, of bullfights and the tragic theatre. Bullfights are not plagued by the unbearable unities that
rule the psuedoclassic tragedies, and, in them, death is
real. The bull is killed just as a good Christian Spaniard in the good old days really used to kill an infidel
dog.

The effect of all this is to create for many, perhaps
for my American friend, an atmosphere that is hard to
breathe, acrid. But once one has gotten used to it, other
atmospheres seem insipid. It is like the austere beauty
of the frozen wilderness. He who tempers his soul or
distempers it—I do not know which—in the contem-
plation of bloody drooping Christs is not afterwards attracted by others.

And that hate, that hate which circulates here everywhere like subterranean lava, that very hate . . . rises
from our very depths; we hate, not one another, but ourselves.

"But you do not have any true love of life, although
you may be attracted by it," another foreigner, a Frenchman, said to me once as if he were making a discovery.
And I answered, "Perhaps." He exclaimed, "What you
really have is a cult of death." I replied, "Not of death,
of immortality!" The fear that if we die, we shall die
entirely, attracts us toward life, and the hope of living
another life makes us hate this one.

La joie de vivre. This has been translated as: The
joy of living. That is only a translation. Say what you
will, it is a Gallicism and not pure Spanish. I have never
read it in any of our classics. Because man's greatest
crime is to have been born. It certainly is!

And that same literary ferocity with which writers,

biting and clawing, skin and rend one another, has its acrid voluptuousness for the one who witnesses it. In that struggle our faculties are tempered. Many of our greatest productions have risen through clouds of defamation. And they still have the bitter taste of their origin. They smell like hate. And the public, as soon as it gets a whiff of hate, is overjoyed and applauds. It applauds just as when it smells blood in the bullring. Blood of the body or blood of the soul, what is the difference?

Is this cultured, is it civilized, is it European? I do not know. Is it ours? Well, can a leopard change its spots? We should be concerned about Schopenhauer deep admiration for Spaniards. What was in him a reflection of German pedantry, an academic position, may be in us an intimate living passion.

Should we be ashamed? Why? Rather, we should penetrate, study, and understand completely this hate we bear for ourselves. We must not ignore it. Once we see it as it really is, as self-abhorrence, even then it will have started to change into something noble, strong, and redeeming. Are you not mindful of that terrible Biblical paradox that bids one hate his parents, his wife, and his children and take the cross, the bloody cross, and follow the Redeemer? While this hate for ourselves passes unnoticed, ill defined, purely instinctive, almost brutish, it engenders egoism; but as soon as we see it as it is, well defined and rational, then it can engender heroism. There is rational hate; yes, there really is.

And there is a Christ, triumphant, celestial and glorious; the Christ of the Transfiguration, of the Ascension, who is on the Father's right hand, for the time when we shall have triumphed, for the time when we shall have been transfigured, for the time when we shall have ascended. But here, in the arena of this world, in this life which is but a tragic bullfight, here the other, the livid, scarred, bloody, drooping Christ.

Rascal And Scat

After many a scrap, Rascal, the dog, and Scat, the cat, mutually agreed that it behooved them to discuss peace. Both were born philosophers and like born philosophers knew that battles with their clawing and biting should precede the discussion with its mewing and barking. Men, who are unnatural philosophers—I do not know whether they are against, above, or below nature—come to blows, after having exhausted their tongues, but they should do just the opposite. How much better it would be for us to begin with the flogging, and when our arms were tired by the beating and our bodies bruised by the blows, we should then stop and discuss our differences! This is true, because all discrepancies in opinion and meaning are but pretexts for quarreling with each other. Let's quarrel, then, in the first place, and perhaps we shall discover that we don't care a rap about the pretext.

Rascal and Scat, the former well scratched by the latter, and the latter well bitten by the former, began to talk things over calmly and nobly. Rascal was a street urchin; Scat was a house cat.

"The street," said Scat, "is the school of the vagabond and of servitude; the ditch makes slaves. There you live at the mercy of each passer-by, and you have, actually, as many masters as there are people who pass. The street is democracy, and democracy is servitude and envy."

"The house," Rascal answered her, "is the school of idleness and excessive pride; the hearth develops ingrates. Within the house you become unsociable. You become fond of the house itself, its walls, its nooks, but not man."

"Oh, my dear friend Rascal!" exclaimed Scat, "don't you know that it is not man himself, but his works, that are worthwhile and useful? The house is worth more than those that built it and live in it. Man has importance in nature because of his works. I assure you that, when he has constructed enduring dwellings, drained swamps, dug canals, when he has made the world inhabitable, he will disappear, leaving behind him only the truly useful and lasting part of all his inventions and contrivances; that is, the part that we, whom he calls irrational, can use. All the rest only flatters his insatiable vanity. The stove in my master's house gives much more heat than his heart."

"I am canine; all that is canine concerns me," didactically added Rascal.

"Were you referring to the human heart?" asked the cat.

"I don't know why I said it," answered the dog.

And Scat:

"That's the way you do in the street, speak without knowing why or wherefore, speak so as not to be silent. There's nothing like the warmth of the hearth to make one meditate."

"If we all should stay at home . . ." Rascal began.

And Scat broke in with these words:

"Life in the street has taught you, as you must admit, to judge words as men do. Believe me, my friend Rascal, ambiguity is a human invention. Staying in a house doesn't imply what men think it does, just as roaming the street, forming a part of the crowds in the squares and joining the mobs, is not participating in public affairs. From his house, without ever leaving it, one can very well govern a city."

"A cat perhaps; but not a dog," answered Rascal. "In houses people become lonely, dogmatic, and fanatical. You cats, following your feline instincts, turn the hearth into an ambuscade, and the whole city becomes a place to seek prey. There are many public bandits, thieving Toms, who turn out to be, at the same, excellent fathers. Their wives absolve them, since the wife who has no civic feeling, forgives the one who robs the city to enrich the family. And you cats, house cats—it has been said a thousand times—have a feminine nature."

"And you dogs," Scat answered, "according to that, have a masculine nature. A currish, cynical, shameless nature. I am not concealing the fact that I like woman better than man; her spirit is more independent, and although she is weaker, she is less servile. The slave is always more slavish than his wife. She knows that she can enslave her master; she is conscious of the strength of her weakness. And this feeling of intimate independence, of profound liberty, grows stronger in the house. Liberty is domestic, not civic; a product of the home, not the street."

"Did you notice, my friend Scat," Rascal exclaimed, "did you notice how dogmatic and cocksure you were?

Do you think anyone is going to like you if you are like that? Do you expect men to like you?"

"I have never tried," answered Scat, "to make men like me. I remember what one of them named Seneca said: 'Why do you rejoice because you are praised by those men that you cannot praise in return?' I don't want applause from men, for I am not going to applaud them, nor could I conscientiously. There are times when I am so nauseated by the odor of them and their wretchedness, that I have to leave their house, I mean, my house, and go out to get a little fresh air."

"That's where the street comes in handy," Rascal interrupted.

"Not the street but the roof, where there is more light, more air, more sky, and more liberty. When I leave the house, when I leave the kitchen, I take a walk on the heights, which are cleaner than the streets where men throw their filth and where the rain produces mud but no flowers."

"Yes, and there," said Rascal smiling, that is, wagging his tail gently, "you have a good time chasing birds. The other day I saw you just at dusk at the edge of the roof, almost lying in the gutter, clawing at the martins as they flew by almost touching you. Did you catch one?"

"One could expect that question from a dog, my friend," replied Scat. "Did I catch one? What of it? Or do you think that we cats hunt for the sake of the prey, as you dogs do? No. For us the chase is a sport not a trade. They couldn't make a hound or a retriever out of a cat as they do with dogs. Liberty is only true liberty in sport; applied to a trade it becomes servitude.

There is only one way to be truly free, and that is, to play, sport; the search for bread and prey is, no matter what form it may take, always servitude."

"But, Scat, don't you believe that dogs play?" questioned Rascal.

"Yes, you do play," said Scat, "games that you learned from men; you play to deceive men and flatter them. Your games are street games. When you are frisking around with each other, I always think that you are jumping through hoops or walking on two legs. Walking on two legs! That is a slavish posture! Your head up, that is, looking into your master's eyes, waiting for the watchword. No, not that; one must always look at the ground, for the ground is the guarantee of liberty. A vertical spine is easily bent."

"What nonsense, friend Scat, what nonsense!" exclaimed Rascal. "Is there anything more noble for a cat or a dog than to take man as a model and be like him? Perhaps you don't think that man is the crowning glory of the animal kingdom?"

"I suspected," answered Scat disdainfully, "that you tended to be a philanthropist. I should have guessed it from your servility. Man, the crowning glory of the animal kingdom? He is conceited enough to believe it. But the animal kingdom, or better, republic, does not have one glory but as many as the species that compose it. It ascends and perfects itself in a thousand places. Now men are talking a lot about *superhuman* things. Well, the ideal of the dog should be *supercanine,* and that of the cat, *superfeline,* and not man. Your remote ancestors, living in the forest, friend Rascal, used to howl; then, after they had begun to associate with men, they started to imitate him, and when they tried talk they barked. Do you think a bark is better than a howl?"

"It sounds better to us," said Rascal.

"Your ears have been spoiled by your association with man," answered Scat, "but when you are really in trouble you don't bark, you howl. Barking is only a vile imitation. And perhaps our meowing began the same way. Dogs and cats are being ruined by their imitation of man."

"I don't blame man for saying you are ungrateful," observed Rascal. "You are. Ingratitude is a feline vice."

"Ingratitude! Did you say ingratitude?" Scat burst forth indignantly. "Ingratitude? I am fed up with that expression. The person who calls anyone else ungrateful is insolent or hypocritical. Let's not mention how low it is to do favors so that we will be thanked for them; let's not mention that. But, tell me, don't you believe that gratitude can only exist among equals? It is not enough for someone to do us a favor so that we may feel obliged to thank him for it; the benefactor must be like us, there must be a community of feeling between his action and our reception of it. What ridiculous, impertinent man can accuse us cats of being ungrateful? Micifuz could well complain of our ingratitude, and he doesn't; but as for the master of the house where I live, let's consider him. He thinks he is doing me a kindness by letting me eat the scraps and leftovers from his table. The old scarecrow even thinks that I should appreciate him when he strokes my back. So, I am disagreeable! I am ungrateful! Tell me, why must I appreciate those caresses? Do you suppose that he is doing it for my sake? Not at all, he does it because he likes it. He enjoys passing his hand along my spine; let his enjoyment be his reward. Why does he imagine that I should thank him? There is no need to appreciate his caresses or his applause. You jump cleverly through the hoop, they enjoy seeing how well you jump, and applaud you; they are showing their satisfaction, which is reward enough for them. Appreciate their caresses! Call me ungrateful! After all, I am not surprised, because only the young of humankind, only the whelps of man think of calling the girl who does not return their love ungrateful. The son of the master of my house, whose face is homelier than a stump fence and who hasn't enough brains to make a fool of himself, still calls a girl who has turned him down five times, ungrateful. Such is the human idea of ingratitude, and for this reason I feel honored when men call the feline race ungrateful."

"Those theories, friend Scat," said Rascal, "are among those that men consider anarchical."

"Oh, forget about men!" Scat interrupted. "Let men say what they please, but I tell you, Rascal my friend, that those aren't theories or anything of the kind. And as for anarchy, that is another human invention in imitation of the animal kingdom. He, the supposed monarch of the animals, is the one who invented that. But that doesn't mean that it is true in our republic. . . ."

"All right, fine, we can continue some other day," Rascal broke in.

"Yes, I can see that your master is calling you; go and chase him," taunted Scat. "I am going to look up my sweetheart so that we can gossip about men in a sweet amorous tête-à-tête."

"But . . ." Rascal began to say.

And, Scat, guessing his intention, added:

"You are right, our amorous tête-à-tetes are mainly gossip about men. So are all lovers' chats. If you see two couples at two windows, you can be sure that they are murmuring about one another; and if we didn't complain and murmur about men, what could we gossip about?"

"See, friend Scat," Rascal concluded, "how you depend on men as much as I do, and live as his slave? You need him to run down and so that you can boast of your independence. The clawing of your tongue is more slavish than my licking his hand. So is the world. Goodbye, Scat, my best to your sweetheart. My master is calling me."

And they separated.

The Portico Of The Temple

A Rambling Dialogue Between Two Friends, Roman y Sabino.

Roman—What if we haven't invented anything? Supposing we had? Thus we have avoided the effort and excitement of having to invent something, and our spirits are fresher and more vigorous. . . .

Sabino—On the contrary, constant effort maintains the freshness and vigor of our spirits. Genius atrophies and disappears when it is not used. . . .

R.—When it is not used to invent those things? . . .

S.—Any things at all. . . .

R.—Who says that we haven't invented other things? . . .

S.—Useless things!

R.—Who is to judge their usefulness? Don't fool yourself, if we haven't set about inventing things of that kind, it is because we don't feel the need of them.

S.—But as soon as others invent them, we take them over, suit them to our needs, and make use of them; you can't deny that.

R.—Then, let them invent, and we shall profit by their inventions. For I hope and trust that you are convinced that electric light is just as effective here as where it was invented.

S.—Better, perhaps.

R.—I wouldn't go so far as to say that.

S.—But they develop their genius inventing such things and train themselves for further inventions, while we. . . .

R.—While we are saved the effort.

S.—For what?

R.—To go on living, which is a great deal.

S.—But, in addition, science not only has a practical value or an application to life through ingenuity, but it also has an ideal and pure. . . .

R.—Yes, it is the vestibule of wisdom, since through it we form a concept of the universe and of our place and value in it. Science is the portico of philosophy, isn't it?

S.—Beyond question.

R.—What if the temple of wisdom had, my good friend, a secret back door concealed in its walls, through which one might enter without any door or vestibule?

S.—Perhaps the search for that false back door takes more effort than entering through the vestibule and waiting until the main door is opened.

R.—More work, perhaps, it is true, but work that is more in keeping with our abilities. What is hardest for one, is most practical for another, and vice versa. Besides, if we insist upon entering the dwelling of wisdom through the vestibule of science, we are taking the risk of staying in it all our lives, waiting for the main door to be opened, and frankly, my friend, if I am going to stay outside, I prefer to stay in the open air, under the sky and the stars, where I can feel the breeze directly.

S.—You are trying to find excuses for laziness and idleness.

R.—Did you say idleness? Look, hand me that

book, the one on your right, that's it, the *Sermones del P. Fray Alonso de Cabrera* that have just been published in the "New Library of Spanish Authors." Let me have it. Here it is, in the first sermon, in the *Reflections on Septuagesima Sunday* concerning that text in Matthew (XX, 6) "Why stand ye here all the day idle?" Listen to good father Dominico as he defends the monks and abbots against the accusation that they earn their living by singing and are idle throughout the year, recalling the definition of Saint Thomas, his religious brother, to the effect that leisure is the opposite of an order directed toward achieving its own effect. And as one would expect, he calls idle all those things that are not used in achieving things that lead to their common end, which is their salvation. "If your preoccupations, concerns and affairs separate you from God, you are idle, you are a vagabond and a loiterer," he says.

S.—And do you, yourself, agree with that?

R.—I neither approve nor disapprove of anything. I am only saying that many stand in the portico of the temple, without any expectation of entering some day, in order to protect themselves against the weather, and because they cannot stand the direct rays of the sun or the open air. I am only saying that many are not seeking the cultivation of science but a narcotic for life; that the madness with which men and peoples are giving themselves over to what they call civilization, is only the result of their desperate anxiety not to fall into what we call barbarism.

S.—And what of the back door, the secret escape?

R.—Only one who has shed many heartfelt tears can discover it. "Love is born," the Idiot says in his *Contem-*

plations, "like tears which fall to the breast from the eyes, because love is born from understanding and falls to the heart through faith." But I think that the opposite happens. All the great works of wisdom have been children of true, that is, pitying love. When you find wisdom in a scientific work, you can be sure that it is the result of passion, pitying passion much deeper and more profound than the miserable curiosity to find out the why and wherefore of things. "Ye shall be like God, knowing the science of good and evil," the serpent tempted Adam and Eve when they were languishing in the fatal happiness of the Garden of Eden, without any worries.

S.—And applying this to our country, what do you make of all this? What application does it have to our State? Since with so great and such unjust and harmful disdain you speak of the door of the temple, show us the door of which you are speaking, by which one enters directly without having to pause.

R.—One man cannot show another that door; he can, at most, only awaken in him the desire to seek it for himself. Things of personal intimate experience cannot be transmitted from man to man. We can exchange coins and ideas, but not their enjoyment. Not long ago, in a book by Bernard Shaw, I read this maxim: "The one who can, does; he who cannot, teaches."

S.—You sound like the Krausists; all your time is spent in preliminaries and introductions.

R.—Notice that those who complained most thirty or forty years ago that the Krausists were spending their time in preliminaries, were the ones who spent theirs making indices, epilogues, catalogues, and lists of errata. One is as bad as the other. They have moved, not into the vestibule of the temple, but into its yard, where they are busy at gathering, arranging, and classifying scraps and parings.

S.—All right, and what are you of the open air doing?

R.—We are the solitary ones, and the solitary ones understand each other even without speaking. The solitudes of the other solitary ones accompany me in my solitude. Much is said about solidarity, and we are told all those who live in the portico of the temple and have their shops there feel a common solidarity. Doubtless, they send customers to one another, because they have carefully separated their wares and offerings, and they praise each other's goods. I understand the repugnant family system of those merchants, but I assure you that in the depths of their hearts they are no more closely united than we who wander, aimlessly and fruitlessly, in the vicinity of the temple, under the open sky, seeking a great grief that will open the hidden back door for us. And when at night they close their shops and go to sleep among their trash, believe me, theirs is a troubled sleep, for it is then in the silence that they really get to know each other.

S.—Supposing that some day the doors of the temple are opened wide to them? That is what they are humbly awaiting.

R.—Humbly? Theirs is a fine humility! Their humility is more real than is their salvation. You don't know how those hawkers and peddlers scorn those who make the trinkets that they sell. Humbly! If they were humble, the temple doors would open.

S.—And if they are opened to them?

R.—They will not enter, you can be sure of that. Their

hearts are stuck to the gewgaws of their shops; each one is so well satisfied with being a specialist in rings, or in balls, or scented soaps, or whistles, or old books, that he would not leave his shop even to enter the temple and see the face of God. They are misers and nothing more. Besides, what would they do in the temple? They have forgotten their songs. One doesn't hawk his wares in there; one sings. If they entered, Christ would drive them out with a whip. Let them sell psalm books in the portico, and let them compare them, and study them, and edit them, and correct them, and embellish them, but don't let them go in to sing with them, for Heaven's sake. What connection is there between the two?

S.—Nevertheless. . .

R.—Nevertheless, this old Kempis that you see here on my table, with its text, clean, bare, and ready for battle, has brought me more comfort and consolation than his did to the man who made a critical edition of it, preceded by a most scholarly introduction and followed by very erudite notes, as useless as the introduction. That is but an example of morbid lust for knowledge.

S.—What else do you want them to do?

R.—What else? Lose hope and tell us of their despair or become hopeful and tell us their hopes. Sing!

S.—Not all birds were born to sing.

R.—Well, those who were not born to sing, should not; but neither should they hawk nor pilfer.

Fanatical Scepticism

You tell me that in the society which surrounds you, scepticism is found accompanying spiritual shallowness. That is natural. Those disillusioned youths of twenty-four understand neither life nor its meaning. They cannot understand it because they never made use of it to help another.

You may have heard of the story of the despondent individual who went out one night planning to kill himself. When he was about to carry out his dismal plan he was attacked by two bandits who, intent upon robbing him, threatened his life. Since he was about to kill himself, it would have been natural for him to let them do it for him, but he did not. On the contrary, he defended himself and in doing so killed one of his assailants. He discovered that his attempt to save his own life had cost another his life. He realized its value as soon as he saw at what a high price he had retained it, and gave up the idea of suicide.

If those disillusioned youths had bought their lives at any sacrifice, they would not be sceptics.

To them everything is valueless; there are no chaste women or noble men. Vanity is their ruling sentiment. It is not important for them to be, but to seem to be.

There is something still worse, which is when those youths come to possess an aggressive, fanatical, intolerant scepticism, a scepticism that is dogmatical in its anti-dogmatism. I have met sceptics like those, rabid sceptics. I have known some who became frenzied when anybody affirmed anything, and they in turn were affirming that nothing could be affirmed, which is as truly an affirmation as any other. *Ignorabimus,* we shall be ignorant, is as much a dogma as any other dogma, and it comes more from scientific despair than conviction.

The *ignorabimus* of the agnostics resembles the *lasciate ogni speranza,* abandon every hope, that Dante placed at the door of his hell. The science that is within the inclosure over whose door is *ignorabimus,* is truly infernal on account of its maddening hopelessness and despair.

Never rely upon the false, apparent tolerance of those sceptics or agnostics; those of us who seem confident and dogmatic are much more tolerant. The man who says yes and the man who says no can come to understand each other better than either of them the one who says, "What do I know about it?" The latter is almost on the point of saying, "What difference does it make to me?"

Doubtless you remember that very famous passage in *Acts of the Apostles* when Paul of Tarsus spoke before the tribunal of Athens and those cultured Attic agnostics calmly listened to him until he came to the resurrection of the flesh, but then, they could stand him no longer. That was the limit of their agnostic tolerance.

Sadducean rage is truly terrible. One could say that their souls are filled with despair because they cannot believe or even wish to believe, and when they find themselves facing someone who believes or wants to believe, the bitterness of their despair is loosened; they become satanic, for they say that Satan, being unable to love, goes about trying to prevent men from loving.

Do not believe that the intolerance of believers is the worst. It may assume sharper and apparently more brutal forms, but fundamentally it is more human. The worst intolerance is the intolerance of what is called reason. The most merciless forms of repression of any belief are those used by those who did not believe anything and were using the beliefs of others as an excuse for other aims. Political rather than religious ends made the Inquisition particularly cruel.

But there is another gentle subtle inquisition which, although it does not kill by imprisonment and fire, kills slowly by social ostracism, by hints of insanity, by sarcasm.

I knew a man of science, a true scientist, a specialist of positive and recognized merit in his field, who used to conceal many of his personal beliefs through the fear of being discredited and even scorned by the members of his profession. He was bearing the terrible burden of spiritual barrenness.

Note that we are irritated most, not by the fact that our neighbor has more knowledge or science than we, but by his possessing greater powers of imagination and appreciation.

It is a curious phenomenon, frequently observed, that men of faith often take refuge in satirical writing and say fantastic things, promenading their fantasy, in order to freely express their pent up feelings. They make believe that they are writing in jest what they feel very seriously. The famous doctor, physicist, psychologist, and philosopher, Gustav Theodor Fechner, who contributed so much to several sciences, is a good example of this.

It was Fechner's lot to be active when metaphysics was discrediting itself, after the fantastic visions of the Hegelians. Having as he did a powerful poetical-philosophical imagination, a great metaphysical faculty—for metaphysics is as poetic as scientific—he was able to restrain and revitalize it. His satirical works, some of which are most entertaining, such as *Comparative Anatomy of the Angels* or *Life after Death,* published under the pseudonym of *Doctor Mises,* reveal one of the innermost recesses of Fechner's noble ingenuous soul. Beneath his humorous jesting is much seriousness.

Once I asked a man of science about another man of science, and he answered, "He is hopeless!" When I asked him why, he replied, "Just imagine, he is interested in spiritualism." "Sir!" I returned, "in this way he will be able to try to discover why there are spiritualists in the world, which is a very interesting and scientific problem, regardless of the objective value of spiritualism, which we are not discussing at present." The serious gentleman tried to pin me down by something that he called *reductio ad absurdum,* confronting me with the example of fetichism. I do not take a back seat so easily, especially when dealing with one of those obstreperous negative dogmatists; therefore, I answered that, actually, our inability to become fetichists, even for an instant, prevents our reaching a complete and sound explanation of fetichism.

Nearly all sociologists—those terrible sociologists, the astrologers and alchemists of the twentieth century—nearly all that those obstreperous gentlemen write about savages, suffers because they are unable to become savages or imagine themselves as such. This is a much more difficult undertaking than is generally believed.

The fact a child of seven has not been an adult of forty and on the other hand the forty-year-old was a seven-year-old, leads us to believe that it is easier for the adult to put himself in the place of the child. Nevertheless, I am convinced that for most men of forty it is little less than impossible to imagine how they thought and felt when they were seven. I think that I am one of the men who retains the freshest memory of their youth and, contrariwise, when a short time ago, I was writing *Memories of Youth and Childhood,* which I have just published, I noted how hard it was for me to recapture the attitude of my childish spirit before the spectacles that confronted it.

That variety of stern agnosticism which usually leads to fanatical scepticism in certain men of science, cannot be other than "asympathy," that is, the inability to put one's self in another's place and see things as he sees them.

These people form a sort of tacit freemasonry, and, smiling pityingly and disdainfully, avoid those who journey through life seeking to solve the mystery.

Sometimes one meets one of those obstreperous disillusioned youths and discovers that they know for a fact and beyond any doubt, that when we die we die completely and that all this business about the possibility of a future life in any form whatsoever is an invention of priests, old ladies, and humble spirits. Then, to console you, they come out with their idea that nothing is lost, only changed, and that the atoms of our body—they talk as if they had seen them—go to form other bodies, which repeat our actions, and I do not know how many more pleasantries, which console us as much as the discovery of the tuberculosis bacillus consoled the consumptives.

Those kind gentlemen have marked the boundaries of human knowledge saying: "Beyond here is nothing but darkness and confusion."

Mystic! Here is a word of which at present I do not even know the approximate meaning. There are others in the same category, for example: modernist, democrat, progressive. I do not understand the term mystic. I know only that in some peoples' mouths it is a means of berating others.

Of course, as terrible and as complete as this scepticism, or better still, fanatical agnosticism, is, I prefer it to the scepticism of which you are speaking to me, the kind that accompanies shallowness, the scepticism of those that are disillusioned and surfeited with a life that, as it did not deceive them, could not have surfeited them. Such scepticism is but a demonstration of ridiculous pedantry. Intrinsically it is but the evidence of a cold heart. I might say more correctly not of ice, but of sand.

This reminds me of the very beautiful poem by the English poetess, Christina Rossetti—a chosen spirit—in which she says:

> I dug and dug amongst the snow,
> And thought the flowers would never grow;
> And still no green thing came to hand.
> Melt, O snow! the warm winds blow
> To thaw the flowers and melt the snow;
> But all the winds from every land
> Will rear no blossoms from the sand.

FANATICAL SCEPTICISM

There is nothing more terrible than frivolity, superficiality, that is, sandiness. Those sophisticated people whose only preoccupation is what they call society life have souls of sand. In any country where they come to predominate it is time to tremble.

How a man of passion and faith suffers among such triflers! And the more he is recognized, the more he suffers. Don Quixote's martyrdom reached its peak amongst the festivities held in his honor by the high society of Barcelona. One should read, in the study on Carlisle that Burns included in his book on heroes, what he has to say when the good Scotch villager came to be the spoiled child, that is, the plaything of the high sosociety of Edinburgh.

The worst thing that can happen to a man is for him to get to be in style among such people.

If you happen to be familiar with the marvelous sermons of that man of God named Frederic William Robertson, read the one that he delivered in Brighton, November 7, 1852, on the scepticism of Pilate and, in general, read everything that he said in his sermons about the superficiality of sophisticated people. Egoism is more easily found among shallow, sophisticated people than among people who perhaps have once or twice been found guilty in court.

On Obscenity

Two days ago the Madrilian newspaper *Correspondencia de España* published a very interesting and just article by Maeztu on the Spanish Watch and Ward Society.

He begins with a translation of the severe criticism that Doctor Horton made of the illustrated advertisement of *Life,* a gazette that was going to be published in London.

Horton says:

"I wager without any hesitation that no decent person will speak a single word in the defense of such a publication. It can satisfy nobody, unless he is a moral imbecile or a cretin in decadent civilization.

"Let the editor, the contributors and the illustrators of this publication come out of hiding. They would blush if their mothers ever saw them. Any gathering of decent Englishmen would loathingly disdain them, after having covered them with insults and jibes. How can a great community like ours allow paper to be sold in this form? If bookstores and news stands do not have enough moral fibre to disdain them, the law must intervene. If it cannot be done by law, then public opinion must speak. A publication of this kind does more harm than the most immoral acts in the street. Why do we quarantine physical ailments and destroy the infected garments? To save the community from death. Well, a publication like this one is an infectious disease; it exists to spread an evil strong enough to destroy the strongest nations. People who exploit in this way the harmful elements of human nature and conscientiously set themselves to corrupt youth should be imprisoned and quarantined. They are a public danger."

At the end of this criticism by the English doctor, Maeztu comments upon it in reference to Madrid, observing that the life of *Life* will be short. He says:

"You probably believe that Doctor Horton's criticisms appeared in a violently reactionary and clerical periodical. Not at all. They were published by *The Daily News,* a radical, anticlerical, and almost socialistic publication; the most progressive daily in London."

And he proceeds to ask that a Watch and Ward League be formed in Madrid, composed of people of the most widely varying political beliefs.

There was a parents' association, but they were parents of exalted Catholic families and, in addition to persecuting immorality, they persecuted heresy.

The fact is, and I am sorry to say it, that in Spain it seems as if the campaign against vice has been solidly linked to the reactionaries. And this is one of the reasons why liberalism is discredited among clean-minded people. A friend of mine recently said to me, "You know that I am and have always been a liberal, believing in true liberalism, as you would say, the kind that is condemned by the Pope. You know that I believe in freedom of conscience, of religion, of the press, etc.; but, my friend, how can I join the liberals here if most of them are very indecent in their conduct?" I recalled immediately—my friend was a Basque—that I shocked certain liberals in

Bilbao who were entertaining me at a banquet, when I said that liberalism would never be effective until it was spearheaded by a strong nucleus that went to bed at ten, drank only water, and had no mistresses.

Maeztu is quite right in saying that it is not a question of clericalism or anticlericalism, but of the physical and mental vigor of future generations. Lust stultifies; chastity and sobriety strengthen both heart and mind. I have always believed, and I have said so on many occasions, that Don Juan Tenorio was a complete idiot.

Doctor Horton, in his biting criticism, speaks of moral imbeciles and of moral talent. And so it is; virtue is a form of intelligence, and vice is either foolishness or madness. Almost all the drunkards, woman chasers and gamblers that I know lack the spiritual vigor necessary to undertake noble enterprises, which yield far more exquisite and deep satisfaction than do vicious pastimes. The increase of gambling in any country indicates a mental weakening. I shall speak of this later.

Maeztu speaks of the sad spectacle that Madrid has presented for some time, with its pornographic weeklies, and those theatres and night clubs where a miserable dancer bellows indecencies and teasingly discloses her God-given stock in trade, as the audience, a dirty, stupid, brutish audience, roars like an animal in heat. And if these places were closed, what wouldn't our liberals say?

Maeztu wonders if the Watch and Ward Society would be opposed and adds:

"It would not encounter opposition now among those writers who ten years ago would have opposed it in the name of paganism and of liberty. Liberty of conscience cannot be classed with pornography. And, speaking of paganism, we cannot judge it by one aspect. Further, is there any proof that it ever had a pornographical aspect? In a pagan civilization, why should we not admire physical strength? Let us be strong, and then, if anyone so desires, let it be called pagan.

"Let us see to it that our youths reach the age of twenty as strong as possible and then let them do what they will with their strength. But, first, let them be strong and, above all, may they not be lascivious."

That is fine, and much better coming from the pen of Maeztu, who is one of those that have contributed most in Spain to the popularity of Nietzsche, that sworn enemy of Christianity.

Hapless Nietzsche, poorly read and worse understood, and the humbug, D'Annunzio, with their counterfeit paganism, have corrupted much of our youth, which has been led to recklessness by the first, and to vice by the second.

As Kidd maintains in his *Principles of Western Civilization,* the motive force in the development of culture, the *raison d'être* of human civilization, is the sacrifice of present generations for those of the future, the preparation of the future. And all those doctrines of moral or practical materialism see only the present in relation to the past. Peoples that come under its sway degenerate and disappear, barred from reproducing themselves by scepticism or mechanical means.

For some time a group of decrepit striplings has constantly been bombarding our ears with their talk about life and repeating that those of us who do not feel and think as they do are sad, gloomy misanthropes who hate life. The main joy of their lives seems to be saying that they are joyful and shouting from time to time, "Long live joy; long live license", or some other bit of nonsense. They resemble those stupid, ridiculous characters in *Genio alegre,* that play by the Quintero brothers, whose happiness—I am referring to the characters and not to the authors who, I believe, are honorable, serious, hard-working, clean-minded young men—whose happiness, I repeat, consists of clapping, laughing, and saying that they are happy. They are no happier than I am.

It is evident that joy is not linked with vice, and that vice is really sad, as is everything sterile; but I am not the first to mention these ideas.

And in respect to paganism, there is so much to be said. . . .

Maeztu neglected to speak of the general attitude here in connection with lust, and to point out that the prevalent conception of liberty is possible only when the meaning of Christianity has been forgotten. He could have mentioned, also, that the English moral sense stems directly from the vigor that the Reformation gave to Christianity there. Among the non-Catholics or the anti-Catholics, it has been the fashion in Spain to repeat all the nonsense that the ignorant, the superficial, the licentious, the insane, and the pessimistic have muttered against Christianity. We have been flooded with anti-Christian booklets, usually translated by disreputable authors, booklets like *Religion for All,* or a certain collection of follies called *Jesus Christ Never Lived,* or something of the like. The serious thoughts of the non-Christians with a calm and just spirit have not been made available.

Moral fibre is very widely scattered among us, and

there are many persons who consider themselves cultured because they bathe daily, but whose souls are filled with filth.

There will surely be many men of the world, club members—he who cannot be anything else is a club member—who will smile when they read these stale Puritanisms and who will say, "It is easy to tell that this poor fellow lives in an old Castilian city with his nose in his books." Let me inform them, in advance, that, impossible as it seems, I, too, have been in Paris, whither I am not at all anxious to return.

Others will ask, "What does society or worldly life have to do with lust and vice?" I am ready to admit that neither ballroom dancing nor flirtation is an orgy, but I know what I mean and they, also, understand me.

The increase of licentiousness here is due to the absence of high, fecund ideals, to the lack of religious interest, to the nonexistence of deep spiritual preoccupations, to the death of romanticism. The expression *joie de vivre* and that false pseudopaganism were invented by the same ones who proclaim the falsity of every serious work. Those who are enraptured by Marcel Prevost are incapable of reading any deep serious thinker.

Willy's *Claudinas,* which have been translated into Castilian and have been very popular, are not only corrupting the moral sense, but also are idiotizing our people. The one who is amused by their coarseness has a mind, to put it simply, of the lowest quality. I shall not comment on those books that are written for adolescents and old men in their dotage.

A Watch and Ward Society, as Maeztu proposes, is all very well, but that Society should concern itself with every form of worldly superficiality, including that unhappy tendency to turn everything into *sport.*

Between the English sportsman as I conceive of him, who strives to strengthen both body and will, undergoing privations if necessary, and our ridiculous *sportsman,* whose *sportsmanship* prefers gambling to the chase, there lies an abyss. I shall discuss this later in greater detail.

There is an intimate relationship between vice, superficiality, antireligious sentiment, *sportsmanship,* and the belief that civilization is measured by toilets, paved streets, railroads, and hotels.

"How Spanish this all sounds!", someone will say, and I shall answer, "Would to God that it were!" Unfortunately it is not today, except perhaps in some isolated sector such as my blessed Basque country, where, to our great fortune, there is a sentiment very similar to that so unjustly censored English *cant.* The cynics say we are hypocrites; let God, who sees us both, judge us.

Nobody can dissuade me from the belief that only temperate peoples are able to play a glorious role in human history, and that they alone will be able to contribute to an enduring civilization. Lust, gambling, and drunkenness stultify a people and brutalize man. If, for every school that is opened, a gambling den, a brothel, and a bar are not closed, the school is useless.

Popular Materialism

I spent Easter in Valencia this year, upon the invitation of the medical students of the University, who had asked me to take part in the ceremonies in celebration of the one-hundredth anniversary of Darwin's birth.

It turned out to be a very enjoyable occasion for me, especially because it was, more than anything else, another demonstration of the broad spirit of liberty that is gradually embracing all Spain, and of the deep respect that our Government has for opinions.

When the professors from Bordeaux arrived, one of the things that surprised them most was the sight of a placard in the street inviting Republicans to a banquet commemorating the thirty-sixth anniversary of the proclamation of a republic in Spain. "Is not Spain a monarchy? How does the Government permit this?" They kept asking, and finishing with *"c'est etonnant!"* It is a fact that today in violently sectarian France such a thing would not be permitted. They were astonished by all that we told them concerning the very great, almost unlimited, liberty of teaching whatever he may wish, which is enjoyed by the Spanish professor. It is apparent day by day, let the short-sighted ones who keep shouting "Clericalism! Clericalism!" say what they will. Spain is one of the freest countries in the world.

At least as far as the Government and the authorities are concerned. In the Medical School of the University of Valencia they have erected in the most visible spot in the building a tablet which reads: "To Darwin, the Valencian medical students, on the first centenary of his birthday, February 14, 1909." Would they permit the Catholic students of any French university to set up a tablet to a leader of orthodoxy, even one of the greatest and purest?

If there is a lack of liberty here, it is below, among the people, in customs, in widespread social affairs; not in the Government, in laws, or in politics. Here the Government is much more liberal than the people.

This popular intolerance is everywhere, just as evident among freethinkers as among Catholics.

Few things are more sad and lamentable than Spanish "freethinking." It reminds me of an amusing caricature suggested by the present French circumstances; these words are underneath: "Here you must not think freely. Here you must be a freethinker!"

Nobody has preached culture and its diffusion more than I, but nevertheless there are times when I lose my faith in it, or at least when I doubt that the best way to spread it, lies in teaching people to read, and in their reading.

Yes, at times I wonder if workingmen should be taught to read, when I consider what is read by those who can. Just glance at the book list in a popular store and ask which are the favorite selections.

Among the best-sellers in Spain—and perhaps elsewhere— is *The Conquest of Bread* by Kropotkine. It is so fallacious and fantastic that it cannot stand the slightest examination by anyone at all versed in political economy. Another best-seller among the populace, to my great surprise, is Darwin's *Origin of Species*.

I am not placing the important work of the very wise, prudent, and discreet Darwin in a class with that of Kropotkine. Darwin was a calm, prudent, thoughtful man, not in the least dogmatical or sectarian, a true scientist. But his work can hardly be understood by laborers and, with its lack of literary style, must not be very enjoyable. Darwin was not a great author, and Kropotkine's writing is lively, pleasing, and excellent.

What are the laborers who read Darwin seeking? Science? I doubt it. They are seeking—it must be stated—antichristian sentiment; they are beyond the anticatholic stage. And, of course, they do not find any. They are trying to find proofs of their descent from monkeys, an origin that seems flattering to them—I do not find it distasteful—solely because it conflicts with what the priests say. Perhaps there is a worse reason.

It is really a sad thing to know that men who are unaware of Pythagoras' theorem, the method of solving a simple numerical proportion, the location and functions of the liver, the law of gravity, the cause of the seasons, the composition of the atmosphere, in short, the most elemental elements of the sciences, start out by reading works which take this knowledge for granted. Science is not the object of their search; they seek a form of pseudo-philosophy with more or less scientific roots. which is manifestly antichristian and even irreligious. And they read such superficial and sectarian things as Haechel's sorry book on the enigmas of the universe.

This whole business of popular philosophy makes me tremble. There is no such philosophy.

Ritschl, the great theologian, said very correctly that the attacks made upon Christianity in the name of a supposed science have their origin, not in science, but in a certain pagan religious feeling which uses it as a cloak. They are dictated, not by the scientific conception, but by the pagan religious conception.

In my frequent journeys through towns and cities, when not in my official capacity, I usually use my listeners as guinea pigs; I make tests on them and observe how they respond and react to my words. I have noted that every time they hear me say something which they believe, although incorrectly, implies a denial of the immortality of the soul and of the existence of another life beyond this world, they break into applause. This applause saddens me, and more than once I have turned against it.

If this applause meant: "Fine! Bravo! This is a real man. This man puts his love for truth, however it may pain us, ahead of his desire to console us." If this applause meant this, I would still accept it, although sadly. But no, this applause means quite differently: "Fine! 'Very fine! We don't want another life; this one is enough!" This grieves me because it is an explosion of the most degrading materialism.

The person who does not believe that there is a God or that the soul is immortal, or the one who believes that neither is there a God nor is the soul immortal—believing that there isn't any is not the same as not believing that there is—seems respectable enough to me, but the person who does not want them to exist is most odious to me.

Especially to me, always conscious of that thorn in the depth of my heart; to me, never able to resign myself to stop thinking even for a day; to me, with my longing for eternity. That applause crushes my heart. I can understand a man's not believing in another life, for I, myself, can find no proof of its existence; I cannot understand his being resigned to it and, what is worse, not even desiring another life.

Add to this, those coarse attacks against Christ and Christianity; all that unnatural nonsense which has debased the human spirit, and that growing accumulation of vulgarities always so eagerly devoured.

In one of those popular libraries which arouse and seduce the coarsest instincts of the uneducated masses, there is a certain book, translated from the Italian, which bears the title *Jesus Christ Never Existed,* or something like that. It is one of the most deplorable, confused, and insubstantial books ever written. It was inspired, not by the love for truth, but by the most shameless sectarianism. I was discussing it with a person who had been enraptured by it and I told him, "Its thesis does not shock me. The thesis which denies the historical existence of Christ, claiming that it is only a myth, has been put forward more than once, and with arguments that seem very plausible, or at least with emphasis—most recently by Karthoff—; but it is a thesis destroyed by the most serious investigators, regardless of their ideas." He answered, "I am sorry, because he must never have existed." I, of course, had nothing to answer.

That lack of ideality, that dryness and poverty of inner life, which prevents one from thirsting for another and better life; all that practical materialism saddens the spirit of one who meditates a little upon the value of human life. As for me, I have scant hope for peoples of whom this comes to be characteristic.

Understand me well, I repeat I do not nor can I affirm the existence of another life; I am not myself convinced of it; but my head just does not have room for the idea that a man, a real man, can not only resign himself to not participating in a life beyond, but also renounce and even reject it. The whole idea that we live on in our accomplishments, in our children, and in memory, and that everything is renewed and transformed and that we shall keep on doing our part toward forming a more perfect society—all these things seem to me like very poor subterfuges to escape the depths of despair.

This is why I am distressed by the radicalism of some of our populace and why I expect nothing constructive from it. The radicalism of the Spanish, and perhaps of the other so-called Latin, or to be exact, Catholic, peoples is wanting in religious substance and vitality. The weak point of our socialism is its incorrect notion of the supreme end of the life of the individual.

Let's improve man's economic condition—fine! Let's do away with poor and rich—agreed! Let's arrange things so that with a moderate amount of work we can satisfy all our needs—very well! And what then? We shall have a society such as the one of which Bebel and Kropotkine dream. What will be the lot of each one of us in it? What will be the purpose of such a society? What shall we live for?

"Get rich!" the Calvinist Guizon used to say to the French middle classes. Get rich! Fine! And afterwards, when we are rich?

A country where people think only of getting rich,

114

is a country, . . . I refuse to consider what it would be like. It is enough for me to say that if I were in it I should die from cold, from shame, from loathing.

And as repugnant as I would find the country where getting rich was the sole preoccupation, even more so would be the country in which the main preoccupation was to enjoy oneself, to have a good time, that is, make oneself giddy.

A common patriotic enthusiasm, an imperialistic instinct, the desire to influence other peoples and put one's own stamp upon them is something after all. But this enthusiasm, this instinct, and this longing live among and motivate those peoples that retain an intimate religious sentiment, those people that still preserve an inextinguishable thirst for immortality.

The people that is content with this life lives, frankly, on the defensive, and the one that lives on the defensive will finally be dominated and absorbed by the aggressive ones, by those with a dominating instinct. The so-called struggle for life is effective only when it is a struggle to predominate, not to preserve. The essence of being, rather than the effort to keep on being the same, as Spinoza taught, is the effort to be more, to be everything, is the longing for infinity and eternity.

I do not know what to expect from peoples whose sensibilities have been dulled by a prolonged education in implicit Catholic faith, in routinary beliefs, and which seem to have lost the intimate motivation, the deep restlessness which characterize the most genuinely Protestant spirits. I do not know what can be expected from peoples whom centuries of a religion more social than individual, with more ritual, ceremony, and display than intimate soul-searching meditation, have led into a state of freethinking characterized by indifference and resignation to this vile life.

From the superstition of an infantile and ridiculous heaven and hell they have fallen into the superstition of a coarse, materialistic world.

This is the most important of my cantatas. I know that it will be resented by many, especially by the aestheticians and the militant pagans and by a few poor fellows who, thinking that they are poets, go about humming about Life and Beauty. Nor should I forget the Neoepicureans who know nothing of Epicurus, certain radical seditionists, and others of similar brand; but everyone is born with his battle before him, and perhaps it is the battle that makes him what he is. I well realize I am making myself obnoxious to many, but a good friend once said to me; "If you wish people to respect you in the last half of your life, spend the first half in making yourself displeasing."

In addition to all this, my style of writing is considered by those pleasant fellows. What do they discover? Horrible! It has no style because it isn't a style and observes no conventions. At the moment I am reading two authors, Thucydides and Benvenuto Cellini— each in his own language—, and they both bear me out in my style, thus, just as one who is speaking or dictating, without looking around or turning his ear, conversationally, naturally, like a man and not like a writer. I do not want it said about me that I speak like a book; I want my books, all my works, to talk like men. I want no acoustic effects at the expense of real feeling. If this is art—and it is not—I renounce art and stay with life.

But I am wandering from my subject. I will have another opportunity to say a few witticisms about the already moribund modernists, and especially about those who, with an absolute lack of critical sense and discernment, have more than once taken me as such. This is a hint.

Don Juan Tenorio

Victor Said Armesto, a very alert and cultured young man, who is a professor at the Institute of Secondary Education in Leon, has just published his first, and I trust not his last, book, entitled *The Legend of Don Juan*. Although it is a learned work and a product of Spanish erudition in addition, the book is enchanting.

I say this because in Spain learned works are usually dry, insipid, and disordered. They are notably lacking in imagination, which is equally true of erudition itself. For without imagination, such works are seldom more than encyclopedic compilations of data. Said Armesto observes, quite correctly, in reference to Farinelli's investigations of the legend of Don Juan, that "too much erudition is stifling." And he adds, "An excessive collection of data beclouds the truth to such an extent that, if it does not destroy it completely, it conceals it beneath its showy billowing folds!" Here we should once more be reminded of that German saying about one's being so close to the trees that he cannot see the forest. With the exception of Menéndez y Pelayo, Rodríguez Marín, and one or two others, one must be very devoted to certain studies to read the works of our scholars. It is impossible to read them.

This does not apply to Victor Said Armesto. His book, although a bit redundant and monotonous in spots, can be recommended for its lively style, for the current of animation that runs through it, for the elegance and grace with which it is written, and for a certain waggish, winsome quality, of Galician origin—since its author is Galician—which lends spice to it.

The main object of the book of which I am speaking to you is to combat the impression left by the Italian Hispanist, Farinelli, that Don Juan Tenorio is more Italian than Spanish in origin, that the portrait of the seducer, "has perfect Italian coloring," and that its sources, "must be sought in the very fertile Italian Renaissance." Said Armesto struggles bravely with Farinelli to reestablish the Spanish origin of Don Juan Tenorio, and, in my judgment, the Spanish scholar conquers the Italian. The blows that Armesto directs toward Farinelli's conjectures and suppositions seem to me decisive, and on completing this book on Don Juan Tenorio, the most uninformed reader will, I believe, be entirely convinced that Don Juan Tenorio is genuinely Spanish. By which I, a Spaniard, am not in the least flattered, for I have never worshipped Don Juan.

After reading Said Armesto we are convinced of Don Juan's Hispanism. But let me add that, as far as I am concerned, the famous seducer of maidens, to still more narrowly limit his locale, is Galician more than anything else, even if the author has not mentioned this. Most people think that Don Juan is Sevillian. He has even been confused with that famous Don Miguel de Mañara, in whose epitaph in the *Hospital de la Caridad* of Seville, it says that he was, "the worst man that has ever lived." I was not at all astonished by the observation that Don

Juan seems more correctly Galician than Andalusian.

Undoubtedly the name *Tenorio* or *Tanoiro* is Galician —and not Portuguese as Teófilo Braga holds—and was used as early as the first half of the Thirteenth Century. It comes from the village of San Pedro de Tenorio, not far from Pontevedra. In his book Armesto has included a very scholarly note concerning the Tenorios, whose noble house left many branches, both in Portugal and in Seville. But I, by many indications that have nothing to do with genealogy, am led to think that, if Don Juan was not Galician, at least Galician blood was running in his veins.

It is my supposition, not that of the author, that makes me write these lines. Said Armesto does not go beyond saying that Don Juan was very, very Spanish. The first chapter in his book is called, *Don Juan, a Spaniard?*, and the eighth and last, *Don Juan, a Spaniard.* The task of the book is to dispel the doubt concerning Don Juan's Hispanism, and I believe that it dispels it.

Said Armesto says:

"It is not a trite commonplace, but a very sensible observation, to say that the portrait of Don Juan stems from the deepest and most inborn part of the Spanish race. He is the child of our creative genius, the poetic essence of the ideal that is our heritage; he is the type of Spaniard who stops at nothing and explains to nobody, a joint creation of the national soul and of the epoch. The brilliant, dissipated life of Don Juan, his showy majesty, the impetuous development of his bold, resolute instincts, his lightning-like impressions and suddenness of action, the strong temper of his spirit, at once jocular and inadvertent, his insensate challenges and maddeningly cynical taunts, give us a clear penetrating vision of those young nobles whose idea of law, Ganivet said, was "to carry in their pocket a statutory letter of a single sentence in the following brief, clear, and forceful terms, 'This Spaniard is authorized to do as he pleases' " (Idearium Español, page 64). In such a sense I believe that Don Juan and Don Quijote symbolize Old Spain, the restless, wandering Spain of knight-errantry that had, 'for its law, its courage, and for its decrees, its will'. On one hand, the novelistic nobleman, the heroic idealist, self-denying, sublime, and grave in his madness; on the other, the youthful adventurer, the gay daredevil, the unbridled, frivolous, sensualistic rascal. All the genius of our collective national spirit is represented by those two figures. Don Quijote's ancestral home lies in Castilian Spain, the central part, with its infinite horizon and immense open spaces, tenacious and bold, constant in adversity, desolate and enduring. Don Juan was cradled in Andalusian Spain, the southern part, where the burning sun excites the nerves, with its generosity and ostentation, its spontaneous joy and unchecked love, inadvertent, naughty, and lawless, but always noble, and as careless of its own life as of that of others. The Knight of La Mancha is a deluded idealist whose armor conceals a hero. The Sevillian gentleman is a noble whose cape conceals a rogue."

Where Armesto, in my opinion, best portrays the essence of the character of Don Juan, and of all the Spanish Don Juans, is when he compares him with Leontius of Ingolstadt. I am going to include the passage here because it is, I believe, the most profound and penetrating passage in Armesto's most interesting work. After telling us that Leontius of Ingolstadt is presented to us only as an atheistic, blasphemous, low, impulsive disclaimer, he adds:

"The Spanish Don Juan is neither blasphemous nor atheistic. He is simply a reckless adventurer who, drawn by the joy of the moment, is only remotely conscious of the time when he shall appear at the last judgment; a fiery, rattle-brained, sensual youth, whose egotistic desire for pleasure leaves him no time to think of the proximity of the tremendous expiation. The German Leontius is not in the least concerned about love and women. He is only a violent and impulsive person, a cold, coarse, vulgar unbeliever. Don Juan, on the contrary, is a believer; but he is a believer with unrestrained appetites and sudden resolutions, who, catching a glimpse of happiness, disregards every law and, blinded by passion, rushes to seize it. Don Juan, still very Spanish, never denies the future life; but the remoteness of its justice erases, or better said, banishes any such idea from his mind."

And now, before proceeding to comment upon these very penetrating words, I wish to observe that Leontius of Ingolstadt is not the genuinely German type that should be compared with Tenorio. A happier choice would be romantic, sentimental Werther. And, since they have been contrasted more than once, I am not going to do it again. Especially when I recall how well Stendhal did it in his book *De l'amour*.

Speaking of the Spanish Don Juan again, I believe that, in all that has been said about him, it would be difficult to discover anything more penetrating than that he, "never denies the future life; but the remoteness of its justice erases, or better said, banishes any such idea from his mind." The Don Juan who said, "How long you trust me!" is not, actually, an unbeliever. He affronts the phantoms of the other world, but he believes in it. And this is why he is most repugnant to me, and why I think that he is dangerous for our people. We cannot estimate the harm that is done to us by old repentant Don Juans.

If, like the great Portuguese poet, Guerra Junque — iro, I should write a *Death of Don Juan,* I would depict the professional seducer lying between two monks, after having confessed and having left his fortune, not to the children of his excesses who are running around abandoned and fatherless, but to some monastery, or so that masses may be said for his soul.

Don Juan never questioned the dogma of the church in which he was brought up, because he never seriously considered them. His occupation of chasing and seducing maidens never gave time for such thoughts, or rather, his inability to think about these matters is what led him to chase and seduce maidens. Don Juan is not noted for the depth or inquisitiveness of his intelligence. His conversation is unbearable to all except the women that he captivates.

After having sown his wild oats, Don Juan usually marries and becomes a respectable citizen, full of aches and prejudices, a stubborn, recalcitrant conservative. He hears mass daily, belongs to several brotherhoods, and despises everyone who does not respect the venerable traditions of our ancestors.

In his youth Don Juan was filled with mad unreflecting

courage—better termed confusion than courage. He went from one duel to another, killed several people, and unhesitatingly faced phantoms from another world and invited a stone statue to dine with him. But Don Juan never had the calm, lasting courage to seek the bases of his own beliefs. When he was reminded of the last judgment, he replied, "If you trust me that long . . ."; and said to himself, "I must not think about such things now; the time will come for that".

Those things should not be mentioned in conversation; it is very poor taste to speak about religion in society; it is useless to tire one's brain thinking of one's possible future fate, etc. It is this type of expression that fascinates Don Juans and others of the same ilk. The strange thing is that these Don Juans seem to be bold spirits with strong minds.

Look at Espronceda who seems to me like a Don Juan in more than one respect, be it fact or fiction. Read the charming book *Espronceda* by Antonio Corton—a model biography of a poet—and before you have finished you will have come to the conclusion that, had he not died in his heyday, he would have become Teresa's lover. A politician, doubtless, and a moderate one. Because Espronceda, in spite of the progressive fervor of his early years—a fervor that led to his meeting Teresa Mancha—always carried a reactionary within him, or more precisely, a man who never was willing to fathom certain problems. His famous despair, à la Byron, was chiefly literary and rhetorical. Espronceda could not doubt certain things, because he never thought about them seriously.

I am convinced that our Don Juans, following in the

footsteps of the immortal Don Juan Tenorio, turn to chasing maidens to kill time and fill a vacuum in their spirits, having found no other way to fill it. They are not, like Werther, victims of deep longings of the heart, but slaves of their empty minds.

Or compare him, if you like, with Goethe's other immortal creation, Faust, who, filled with disillusion because science had not satisfied his heart or assuaged his longings, took Marguerite, the immortal Marguerite, into his arms; or fell into hers, which is what really happened, in spite of all appearances to the contrary. We must reread that sublime passage, that passage which is one of the greatest that has ever been written, or will be written, by human hand, that passage where Marguerite asks Faust if he believes in God. When did Doña Inés ever ask Don Juan if he believed in God or investigate the quality of his belief? Even if I am assured that it is so, I shall not believe it.

And they want to present that terrible Don Juanism or something on the same order as the triumph of the openmindedness and freedom of the spirit. The fact is that in the end Don Juan becoms the slave of Doña Inés' confessor, let Tirzo, Zamora, and Zorilla, to mention only Spaniards, say what they will.

How much I would give to have witnessed a meeting between Don Quijote and Don Juan and to have heard what that noble knight of madness, who was in love with Aldonza for twelve years without daring to declare himself, would have said to Doña Inés' fleeting seducer! I am sure that whoever succeeds in penetrating the mystery of that meeting—for it seems certain that Don Quijote and Don Juan must have met at least once—

will bestow upon us the most beautiful page of Spanish literature. I know only one thing and that is that it is to Spain's great misfortune that they did not come to blows, and I do not understand why they did not, because if they had, I am confident that Don Quijote the Mocked would have put an end to Don Juan the Mocker, and it would have been the first time in his life that he had killed a man.

I know more; I know upon what occasion our two nobles met. Don Juan was going to seduce Don Quijote's niece, the well-behaved, domestic, cautious, little niece, who, if she was scandalized by her uncle's acts, would have fainted from the joy of hearing Don Juan's flattery. And it is easy to imagine that, once the knight was dead, Don Juan, a repentant old man, might finally marry the niece to have some one to care for him in his old age. This does not seem so likely, however, when we consider how small was her dowry. For, although old Don Juan is looking for some one to brush his clothes, carry his soup to his bed, put on his plasters, rub him down, and read him the paper to amuse him, he is not unmindful of the dowry.

The thing that I know beyond question is that Don Quijote, nauseated, turned his back on Don Juan in noble disdain, believing that he should not stain his lance on such a man.

Don Juan lives and acts while Don Quijote sleeps and dreams, and this is the cause of many of our misfortunes.

Pseudoscience

The Twilight of Philosophers by G. Papini, a famous Italian writer, is a most pleasing and stimulating, as well as instructive book. The penetrating exactness of its thought is adorned by the pleasant liveliness of its tone. It is, as the author tells us in the preface, "a book of passion — and therefore, injustice — an unscrupulous, violent, contradictory, insolent book like all books by those who love and hate and are ashamed of neither." Do not be alarmed by what the author says about his own book. If you have the opportunity, read it, and I assure you that you will thank me for my advice.

The book contains six carefully reasoned, passionate attacks against six philosophers whose names filled the past century: Kant, Hegel, Schopenhauer, Comte, Spencer, and Nietzsche.

One of the attacks is, as I say, against Comte, and in it, after describing the High Priest of the religion of Humanity with his wavering theological faith in the power of Science, he inserts a paragraph in which he says, "His mysticism of an enamored mathematician could not appeal to the masses or even to the cultured classes, who are more easily fascinated by theosophic occultist priests, and his church, although it has a temple in Paris and a few offshoots in England and South America, cannot be called truly militant or successful."

I can affirm that in South America I know but one

active follower of Comte, and he is a fervent believer in the Master's religion. He is a noble Chilean, who from time to time writes me very affectionate letters filled with humanitarian fervor, not to mention bits of propaganda, in which he is attempting to convert me to the Religion of Humanity. More than once in order to convince me, he has mentioned my Basque origin, but I have never been able to see the connection between the two.

In addition to this fervent Chilean missionary, I know of a positivistic, that is, Comtian journal published in Mexico by D. Agustín Aragón, with the title *Order and Progress,* which goes by the Comtian calendar. (The number now in sight is: "Frederic 10, 118—November 5, 1906.")

Aside from these, I know of no other concrete manifestations of Comtism in Latin-American countries, and my indirect sources of information agree with those of Papini. I have heard that Comtism became very popular in South America, much more so than in Spain, where, actually, even its echo was never heard. A Colombian friend has told me of the influence of Comtian doctrines in the intellectual history of his country.

The relative popularity of Comte has a connection with the respect and admiration which those regions have shown—it is understood that I refer to the few people that are interested in such things anywhere—for another supposed philosopher, Herbert Spencer, whom Papini also derides, calling him an "idle mechanic." The author of the very nonsensical book *The Chilean Race,* written by a Chilean for Chileans, calls him "The Sublime Philosopher" saying that Spaniards and Italians are no longer able to understand him, and consequently, that any blemishes that the Italian, Papini, and I, a Spaniard, find in him are meaningless. Therefore, it is all the better that we are not alone in failing to note the sublimity of the "idle mechanic's" philosophy. The very famous Harvard professor, William James, is neither Spanish nor Italian, but American. He is perhaps the most acute contemporary philosopher, and he has given the "Sublime Philosopher" a terrific drubbing. In his day Stuart Mill, a still greater philosopher, gave him the same treatment.

No reasonably well cultured Italian or Spaniard—let the author of the *Chilean Race* believe what he will—will be surprised that in a psychological work almost half of it is made up of description of the anatomy and the physiology of the human nervous system. There is even one poor Spaniard, unable, of course, to understand the "Sublime Philosopher," whose discoveries in the histology of the nervous system have contributed to the advancement of psychology.

The paragraph by the bright Chilean author who, admittedly, writes only for his compatriots, is but the caricature of a spiritual state that is common everywhere, and especially so among young peoples whose culture is incipient and imported—and since it is imported, is not well rooted—and that spiritual state is sciolism, a blind faith in science.

I call it blind because, the shallower the science of those who possess it, the deeper is their faith in it.

Sciolism is a disease that infects even truly scientific men, especially if their work is very specialized, but it is most prevalent in intellectual mesocracy, in the middle class of culture, in the bourgeoisie of intellectualism. It is common among doctors and engineers, lacking any philosophical culture. It appears in many forms, from the cult of the locomotive and the telegraph to the cult of Flammarionesque astronomy. The happy mortals who live under the enchantment of that illness know neither doubt nor despair. They are as fortunate as professional freethinkers.

In addition to the uselessness of seeking to dissuade them, I wonder if one has a right to snatch from a neighbor an illusion which consoles him for having been born. Besides, to defend himself from our diabolic assaults, he always counters by labelling us "mystic", or "theological," or "paradoxical," or, in extreme cases, "ignorant." He confuses us. Sometimes he feels deeply compassionate toward those who cannot prostrate themselves before science. I have also often felt sympathetic, suffering, in my turn, at my lack of ability to feel any compassion for the one who felt compassion for me. My feeling certainly was not compassion.

William Ellery Channing, the most noble Unitarian, said in one of his sermons, in reference to the fact that if anyone in France or Spain stops being Catholic he becomes an atheist, that, "when false and absurd doctrines are exposed, they have a natural tendency to create scepticism in those who received them without thinking," adding that, "no one is so inclined to believe too little as the one who began by believing too much." So it is with sciolism.

Auguste Comte, as Papini noted, had the soul of a theologian, and his positivism is, basically, as theological as can be imagined. His faith in science was theological and dogmatic but not in the least positivistic. And so, usually, is the faith of his followers.

It is also true that the people who believe too profoundly in science, and more than in science itself,—for this faith is all very well—in the almost absolute value of its aspirations, and that science makes progress—another fetish—and that progress makes human happiness; when these people, I repeat, lose their faith in the science of which they are entirely ignorant or at most only half know, they become the bitterest attackers of true and legitimate science.

Papini says that Comte's best disciples are found in the novels of a great Frenchman, Gustave Flaubert, and that they are Messrs. Homais, Bouvard, and Pecuchet. Undoubtedly the last two, immortal companions, as well as *Madame Bovary's* wonderful druggist, are three of the most typical representatives of sciolism; but another fictional prose character, Zola's Doctor Pascal, is not behind them. With this distinction, that Flaubert's heroes are informed caricatures, since their spiritual father is a man with the very finest sentiments and a clear appreciation of the value of science, a profound scientist himself, whereas Zola's hero is an unthinking caricature, as one might expect from a man afflicted with sciolism as a result of the paucity and baseness of his science and philosophy. Today Zola's scientific pretensions are as amusing as are Victor Hugo's philosophical claims. The solid, reasoned, and prudent doctrines of Claude Bernard, a real scientist possessing as much caution as imagination, passing through Zola's simple clumsy brain, were transformed into the most picturesque and fantastic statements. Similarly, the solid, reasoned, and prudent doctrines of a man as sensible and soundly scientific as Darwin, on passing through certain brains, emerged as oriental fables.

Messrs. Homais, Bouvard, Pecuchet, and Doctor Pascal are most amusing. They do not even suspect the existence of a world other than the one in which they live and die. And if they do suspect it, they imagine that it is a world of pure fantasy, illusions, and mirages, if not of follies.

Add to all this the meddlesome sufficiency of intellectual democracy. I am sure that more than a few of my readers are irritated within, and perhaps without, by the, in my opinion, hardly reverent way with which I have just dealt with Spencer, Zola, and Victor Hugo. They probably have said: "These gentlemen who only seek to differentiate themselves and surprise and amaze us, usually deal openly and scornfully with all those that are recognized and revered by their contemporaries, and on the other hand, they praise others, generally of their own ilk, who are almost unknown." And thus they keep on.

The sciolist or charlatan is, in fact, an intellectual democrat. It is assumed that mental hierarchy is acquired as in politics, by suffrage, and that it is the law of the majority that rules upon a man's abilities, whereby he is exalting himself. Because the basis of such a democracy, and also of any other, is nothing but gratuitous pride, regardless of whether or not an individual has anything of which to be proud. We need do no more than to observe that when they convince a people of its collective superiority, the individuals who most ostentatiously pride themselves on it, are those citizens that have least to point to with pride.

From this gratuitous pride, comes the intimate satisfaction experienced by common souls—and as such, envious—when someone says that superior spirits are bemuddled or that geniuses are mad. The envy of the inferiors and their hidden hatred of spiritual superiority have made them joyfully welcome such doctrines. In his lifetime, Sarmiento was called mad because of envy. That was the vengeance of those that felt inferior to him.

They only recognize and bow to supposed superiority that they themselves have granted and which is only representative. There are a certain number of individuals who owe their fame and prestige to the suffrage of these common, limited intellects. They are representative celebrities. They did not rise above and conquer the intellect of the masses; the masses made them in their image and similarity. And the three mentioned, each in his own sphere, belong in this category. Victor Hugo's loud nonsense was, thanks to his powerfully ardent imagination and the low level and quality of his intelligence, very well suited to arouse the admiration of common spirits and bourgeois mentality.

Spencer's doctrines are within the reach of the man who is most lacking in philosophical education—or even incapable of receiving it. As for Zola, they are few things simpler than the kind of rudimentary psychology that underlies his novels, which do contain an artistic element that is not entirely devoid of value. And so it has happened that those three men have been exalted by the worst one of them, this being undeniably his respective value in spite of the qualities that his fanatical admirers wished to attribute to him. It is natural that neither Leconte de Lisle, nor Stuart Mill, nor Flaubert has been able to equal their popularity. I have chosen three men whose nationality, and to a certain extent, whose age are similar to those of the others.

I shall be asked what this has to do with sciolism. It has a great deal to do with it because sciolism is the faith, not of scientists, but of that haughty and envious mental bourgeoisie that I am discussing, which does not admit the value of anything that it does understand and concedes no importance to all that escapes it. But it cannot deny the effects of the railroad, the telegraph, the telephone, the phonograph, and the applied sciences in general, because that all enters through the eyes. It does not believe in the genius of a Leopardi but of an Edison, another of the idols of that amusing circle.

For them science is something mysterious and sacred. I know one who adores Flammarion, Edison, and Echegaray, and who never pronounces the word Science except with a certain intense fervor and in capitals, thus: SCIENCE! ! ! But the good man—except for this he is a fine fellow—cannot solve an equation and has only the very slight acquaintance with physics, chemistry, and the natural sciences that is required in our ill-starred college course.

Parodying a famous expression, it can be said that little science leads to sciolism and much separates us from it. Semi-science, which is but a state of semi-ignorance, has produced sciolism. Sciolists—be careful not to confuse them with scientists, I repeat—hardly suspect the sea of the unknown that stretches in every direction from the island of science, nor do they suspect that as we ascend the mountain that crowns the island, the sea increases and widens before our eyes. For every problem solved, twenty problems rise to be solved, and as Leopardi said so well:

> Ecco tutto é simile, e discroprendo
> Solo il nulla s'acresce.

Could not a country profit by the presence of a group of these scientific charlatans? Does not their candid illusion prepare the way for and encourage certain undertakings? Is theirs, by chance, an evil that will become a boon? Perhaps, I do not know, but I tell you that I flee from them as from the plague and that there are few people who irritate me and make me lose my patience more than the honorable brotherhood of Messrs. Homais, Bouvard, Pecuchet, Doctor Pascal, and company.

Three Generations

Scene: the dining room of a village inn in my native Basque country; actors: grandfather, son, and grandson; audience: myself, profoundly moved. Three generations of the same family had met there to eat together. The old man, an honorable independent workman, was plain and uneducated, speaking Castilian only with difficulty; his son, a mature man, who in his youth had gone to America where he had made a fortune, married and raised a family, was returning to his native soil to visit his aged father and introduce the grandson; and the grandson, still very young, was a good looking boy, very neat, very finical, and very well groomed, whose careful training was apparent in every move of his knife and fork.

Between frequent draughts of wine, the grandfather was evidencing his joy at the sight of such an elegant grandson, repeating dotingly again and again in his meagre Castilian, "I thought I was going to die without ever seeing you." The father, between the grandfather and his son, between his memories and his hopes, was thinking of God knows what, and the youngster was eating politely and coldly, looking impatiently at his grandfather from time to time as if bored.

That scene was full of meaning, not because of what its actors said, but rather, what they left unsaid.

That pretty youth did not seem to be interested in

anything and was paying no attention to his father's father. They were separated by an abyss. I doubt that he had ever stopped to consider that he owed his good fortune, his education, and everything that was serving as a base for his egoism to the simple, noble, honorable spirit that the old man transmitted to his son, the stalwart toiler who had made a fortune.

Immediately I was reminded that a few years ago I had heard a poor man confess sadly and bitterly that, having amassed a fortune, married and raised a family also in America, he was disdained by his children. "They scorn me," he said tearfully, "they scorn me because I don't speak correctly and because I don't know the things they have learned from the teachers I hired." Later I had the opportunity of meeting one of his sons and I can assure you that he knew less than his father. He could talk about bookish things, jabber a little French and even less English, sigh for Paris, and find fault with his father's people.

You should have heard him constantly comparing our country and the one in which he was born. There was no limit to the superficiality of his comparisons. To him everything revolved around paved streets, water-closets, street cars, restaurants, and theatres. To him civilization meant urbanization and conveniences and, in addition, a certain show of good manners. The real essence of culture was completely unknown to him. He possessed not one grain of poetic feeling or sensibility. He told me that he was not interested in old stones.

Only this lack of sensibility, this want of poetic feeling, or—let us state it clearly—this cold-heartedness can explain certain things. Many an American of Spanish

parents comes to Europe without enough piety, or curiosity even, to visit his parents' fatherland; Paris calls
him. In his father's town, perhaps a tiny village hidden
in the mountains, there are no asphalt boulevards or
electric trollies; above all, there is no *Moulin Rouge* or
chez Maxim. Not all can feel the deep penetrating poetry of one of those little villages.

How beautiful, how deeply pious and poetical is the
account by that great poet, Zorrilla de San Martín, of his
visit to his father's people in the mountains behind San-
tander! Zorrilla de San Martín is a poet, a true poet,
a noble delicate spirit, guarding the treasure of our
secular culture.

I am not known as a flatterer of my country; I could
more correctly be called a bitter critic of its defects. I
have never hidden our weaknesses, but when I happen
to meet one of those pretty youths who find fault with
everything around here, I find myself turning against
them and the superiorities of the lands that they have
come to boast about. Because they both fail to see our
real ills and to comprehend the best features of their
own countries.

One of my neighbors in Salamanca, where I now
live and write, once went to Bilbao, my native city,
and in front of the city hall, a massive, showy, poorly
designed building, he stopped and exclaimed, "I wish we
had something like this in Salamanca." A native of
Salamanca, who has never been near the beautiful old
cathedral of this city except to show it to some visitor,
said this.

At the end of each year I receive many letters spontaneously from my unknown American readers. The

vast majority of them are written in a kindly, amiable tone, urging me to keep on with my work, or, if they do censure me for something, they do it discreetly, honestly, and respectfully. But there are also some, although very few, mostly anonymous, written in a sly, under-handed manner, saying injurious things about me, or more correctly, about my country, its men, and its ways. What nonsense comes from the pens of those artful nitwits. Not long ago I received a letter whose author, after using the term Galician in its derogatory sense—an act which belittles the user more than anyone else—asked me if certain Spanish family names, such as *Iglesias* and *de la Iglesia* originate in foundling asylums, or if they are given to children found in their vicinity.

If I were a spiteful, ill-natured individual, I would have answered that these names and many more had their origin in such asylums, and among them the names of some saints, including the name of San Martín, so justly famous in Argentina.

In my Basque country there has been developing for some time, because of the material prosperity of the region, a most blameworthy feeling of disdain toward those who come there from other parts of Spain to earn a living, working there and increasing the general prosperity of the country. They call them *maquis* and say that they have come there to kill their hunger. That is right, but they also kill the hunger of those that are making sport of them. It is a line of reasoning like that of the factory owner who seriously asserts that he is feeding two or three hundred workers, when it is they who are feeding him and giving him something more in addition.

That poorly disguised hostility toward the immigrant or stranger is a phenomenon that arises when the partner in production becomes a competitor in consumption, when the planting and the reaping are ended and it is time to divide the harvest. It is then that the descendants of the first inhabitants resort to trickery and seek to obtain special privileges as if they had created the fertility of the soil. Is it any merit of mine that my native mountains are filled with rich iron mines?

It is all right for those poor laborers to drag out their lives extracting ore from the depths of the mountains or doing any other work that adds to the wealth of the region; it is all right for them to work. But, as soon as they show any interest in political or social affairs, they are reminded that they came there to work, they are ridiculed for being industrious.

On one occasion an Argentine friend, whose name I had given to an emigrant, wrote me an interesting letter saying, among other things, "Do not encourage ambitious people to come here; we need hands and capital, but not talent. There are too many scholars here in America. In some countries, having nothing else to do, they plan revolutions." I understood immediately what my friend was saying and, by reading between the lines, I understood many things that he did not say. I recalled the bitter tale of a friend and countryman of mine who was a doctor. He suffered a great deal overseas precisely because he was a competent doctor. His learned colleagues outdid themselves to help him . . . suffer.

What have I been led to say by the sight of that family represented by three generations? I can see them yet: the old man striving to use a fork and not his hands as he would have done at home, the youth daintily cutting his meat and peeling his peaches with studied elegance, and between them, the rude man who had made a fortune. I do not know whether he was ashamed to have such a father or such a son or proud of one or the other or of both of them. How well groomed the boy was! How artistic was his head on the outside! I do not know what it was like on the inside but most surely it was furnished with the latest fads from Parisian books.

The mature man, the maker of fortunes, seemed to me to be only the connecting link between his father and his son. And I set about comparing the strong plain old man with the delicate disdainful youth. And, of the two, the old man seemed to be the younger, hardly more than a child. He was probably more than seventy but his was the illusion and the enthusiasm, while the youth seemed to have been born bored and carrying the weight of the greatest disillusionment on his artistic head.

Why was that reunion held in a place as public as the dining room of an inn? Why were those three not before the grandfather's hearth, in the house where the father was born? Perhaps it was on a mountain top whither one had to climb along a stony path, possibly muddy in spots. The youth's delicate feet were only accustomed to smooth macadam and his shining boots had never been spattered by mud. Surely that house did not have even the inn's primitive conveniences. I imagine that in the opinion of the pretty boy with well combed locks it was not a dwelling of a civilized country. For I am almost certain that I know what concept of civilization that scornful, finical upstart had. It was ridiculous and extremely superficial.

No people can progress far until it has lost that concept of civilization which looks upon it mainly as conveniences and facilities for material well-being. Hygiene is important and comfort is more so; but we must agree that among a people that is hygienically careless, the life of the spirit can be far more carefully guarded than among another people that is daily sprinkled with antiseptics. Hygiene itself is indispensable but it should not become a monomania or superstition.

The maxim says: *mens sana in corpore sano,* a sound mind in a sound body, and not *corpus sanum in mente sana;* let us put first things first. Of the two extremes, and they are both abominable, I prefer Job on the dung-heap to a spruce young gentleman whose principal occupation is bathing and perfuming himself.

It is evident that not all the grandsons of our rude, homespun mountain folk feel like the pretty youth I have described; besides, I am glad to believe most of them pride themselves on their ancestry, and if they do not visit their ancestral homes, it is because they cannot and not through laziness. I know all that very well, but I would not like to fail to add my protest against those vain superficial striplings who come here and disdain everything they cannot comprehend, those who judge a people by its manners and who seem to think that the most important agents of civilization are the janitor, the cook, the tailor, and the dancer.

On Lust

Everyone who comes from Madrid to my retreat here in Salamanca tells me that seldom has there been so much pornography in the Spanish capital. The little theaters, and even the large ones, are infested by all kinds of dancers and courtesans of high and low station. Public lust is rising to delirious heights.

For some time now theatre managers have been complaining that their business is declining. The public is fleeing from the theatre, where it is bored by hearing its favorite actors, whose words it knows by heart already, repeat for the thousandth time, the same jokes and the same sentimentalities. It used to be said that the vogue for one-act plays killed the regular drama; later the same thing was said about vaudeville, and now it seems that it is the movies which are killing all three of them. And along with the movies they present all sorts of feminine exhibitions, all more or less naked.

There are some who attribute this in part to the law which regulates prostitution. Since girls under twenty-three years of age cannot be admitted to brothels, those who seek a career based on their bodily charms go on the stage to advertise themselves, and sing or act with whatever ability they happen to have. In this way the theatres are being converted into stock exchanges—the stock being human.

And what scenes, they tell me, are witnessed there

during those performances which no self-respecting lady can attend! What scenes in these performances for men only! The human beast casts off all its inhibitions.

The public roars and howls and demands all sorts of provocative contortions when those poor outcasts dance the *machicha* or other such dances. I have been told that a wealthy spectator, delirious with lust, devouring the dancer with his eyes, exclaimed, "Oh, baby! All I have is yours!"

And all this is happening, naturally, while the public conscience is fast asleep. Rarely has our people's spirit been more apathetic. The gravest things cannot arouse it. Its indifference concerning the most serious problems of social life is terrifying. It might be said that we have no real social life which, basically, is the same as saying that we have no civilization. Social apathy and sexual sensuality go hand in hand.

Whenever many writers speak of liberty they mean the liberty to use women in any way they choose, the liberty of sexual license or free love. Every time that the government tries to check these excesses, they say that it is reactionary and prudish, as if a deeply rooted liberal spirit, believing in progress and freedom of conscience, could not see an ally of slavery in these excesses.

Lust is an ally of tyranny. What moralizing theologians call lust of the flesh usually stifles what the same people call pride of the spirit. Men whose main concern is "to enjoy life"—as if there were only one way to do it—are almost never lofty independent spirits. Almost always they spend their lives enslaved by routine and superstition.

And this is not astonishing. Sexual obsession in an

individual evidences spiritual inferiority rather than superior vitality. Woman chasers ordinarily have a very low mentality and are not troubled by any spiritual worries. Their intelligence is usually on a level with that of a ram, a heavily sexed but notably stupid animal. Here let me mention the story of a widow who, just before she was to marry a handsome, robust young man, was asked if she was not aware of his mental incapacity and retorted, "He's all right for what I want him for."

Consider that braggart, Don Juan Tenorio, and tell me if you know of any character in fiction who says more foolish, nonsensical things. No group of cultured intelligent men could put up with Don Juan Tenorio for more than ten minutes. He must be kicked out. His cockiness and his boasts are nauseating. And you can be sure that if Don Juan Tenorio had lived to a ripe old age, he would have been a conservative defender of the social order and the venerable traditions of our ancestors, and probably a member of some pious brotherhood.

A philosopher once said that in men who love deeply —referring to man's love for a woman—that love is not the main occupation and goal of their lives as it is in those who love little. That, at first, seems paradoxical, but it will not seem so if we examine it more closely. Men with great spiritual capacity—let us estimate it at 100— have a greater capacity for love — perhaps about 20, which means 20%—, while those with less spiritual capacity—let us say 20—even though love demands half of their spiritual interest, or 10, can never approach the depth of love of the former. Bernard Shaw, the clever English dramatist, has said that a woman would always rather possess one-tenth of a great man than all of an ordinary one.

And if this can be said of love in its most elevated form, what can we say of carnal love, or better carnal voluptuousness?

Whenever they tell me that a people or an age is notable for its sensuality and licentiousness, I always feel sure it has been, or is, a people or an age characterized by a very low level of culture.

For a people lust is probably a greater curse than alcoholism, and only comparable to gambling. I have known very intellectual drunkards but, on the other hand, the lewd people that I am acquainted with evidence a general coarseness of thought and feeling. (Let me inform my malicious readers—they are never lacking—that I drink only water, since I am what the English call a *teetotaler.*)

Northern peoples have been called chaste and drunken in contrast with the more voluptuous and abstemious lands of the South. I remember having read, I think in a work by Maeztu, that in the social struggle peoples that are relatively chaste and drunken have the advantage. That seems to me a very dangerous generalization but, admitting that alcoholism is a terrible scourge, it seems to me that its cure is not as remote as that of lust.

An enormous quantity of spiritual energy is squandered and lost in seeking the satisfaction of carnal desire. The greatest advantage of matrimony, and it has many, is that by regularizing his carnal appetite, it quiets a man's excessive restlessness and affords him time and energy for nobler and loftier enterprises. I believe that Tolstoi's son is right in demanding that people marry young, when their sexual life has hardly awakened, living under the protection of both families until they are ready to establish their own households. Not a few evils would thereby be avoided and, above all, young people would retain a great deal of spiritual energy otherwise lost.

Do not think that I take this stand for reasons of a religious nature or on account of any prejudice against things of the flesh. I do like the aesthetic ideal, but it is to make men strong and noble with a wholesome Christian independence.

To be a good man it is first necessary to be a good animal—Spencer is right in that respect—but not animalistic enough to destroy humanity.

I repeat—and I still have many repetitions up my sleeve—that excessive voluptuousness stultifies one's intelligence, and one of man's first duties is to keep his intelligence awake. The man who abandons himself to the pursuit of women, ends by becoming foolish. The tricks that he has to use are the tricks of a fool.

Do not speak to me of passion. Passion is as worthy of respect and, likewise, frequently, of pity, as sensuality is worthy of scorn. Rarely are sensual men impassioned. Don Juan Tenorio was an impassive man; he never experienced a real passion.

History guards the memory of tragic passions. Both legend and fiction have been enriched by tales of famous passions that are already classic.

But neither Othello, nor Romeo, nor Lorenzo de Segura, nor Simon Botelho, nor the knight de Grieux, nor, on the other hand, any historical personage famous for his love, has been especially voluptuous. Unrequited passion leads either to the cloister or to heroism; stifled voluptuousness leads only to boredom or bestiality.

It seems very sad and regrettable to me that carnal license should be linked with the sentiment of liberty. The cause of the religious and civil liberty of the peoples owes more to the Puritans than to libertines. While here, in Spain—I speak of my country because I know it, but what applies to one, applies to others—while here, if there is not a large number of liberals who go to bed at ten, drink only water, do not gamble and have mistresses, things will be bad.

In other countries the parties that are called advanced are those that take pains to maintain a certain air of gravity in their public functions, while it is the conservatives who look kindly upon ethical license, as it favors their plans. Here the conservatives are not noted for their strict ethics; they are content to observe the usual forms. On the other hand, the parties that are called advanced defend license in one way or another. This is in keeping with the coarse, vulgar tone that has always characterized our progressive movement. Few things are actually less spiritual, less civil, and less refined than our progressive movement, and its recent subdivisions.

Thus one of the most harmful prejudices is being formed. Whenever anyone proposes the observance of a certain amount of gravity in our customs, he is immediately labeled a more or less disguised, pious prude.

Once when I was telling my ideas upon this subject to a friend, he turned to me and said, "Well, who is harmed by this? Supposing we consider a man and a woman, both of whom are of age. Should they not be able to do whatever they please?" Confronted by this brutally

logical egoism, I answered, "Nobody can live indepen-
dently; he lives in the society that made him and for
which he should live, and society can and should prevent
a man from making a fool and a brute of himself."

The barbarous antisocial precept that each one can
do as he pleases is one of the causes of our decadence.
Man is a social product and society should, for its own
sake, not allow him to ruin himself. Even if one wants
to make a fool of himself, he should be prevented.

Unfortunate are the peoples among whom lust
abounds! Beyond any question they will eventually be
subjugated by the others who, after reproducing themselves normally, were wise enough to conserve their
bodily and spiritual energies for nobler aims than that
of satisfying their stupid flesh, in order to educate their
children in liberty, truth, and nobility.

Naturalness

Let us begin with an undisputable aphorism, a true analytical axiom which can be expressed as follows: in spirits with an emphatic nature emphasis is natural. I trust that the reader will find this evident, but I also dare to suppose that he will often forget its evidence.

How frequently, actually, does one speak of the naturalness of style, confusing it with simplicity, and supposing, usually erroneously, that simplicity is natural.

The first step, surely, is to understand what is natural and what is not, and we are hardly embarked upon this before we find ourselves confronted with a labyrinth of difficulties.

Somebody added to the old maxim that habit is a second nature, saying that nature is a first habit. Quite evidently the thing that we call one's nature is something that is formed, deformed, reformed, and transformed constantly. And as a matter of fact, we cannot say how anyone is until he has died and death has sealed his personality. What begins by being acquired, in the end is as natural as what is inherited.

In general what the French critics and precept makers call *naturel,* is usually the least natural, at least for us Spaniards, having as we do a most unusual nature which is, in most respects, exactly opposite that of the French. Latin brotherhood is, in this case, as in so many others, nothing but a falsification. It is incorrect to label as brotherhood the influence resulting from proximity, which is almost always harmful.

The niggardly, bigoted French system of aesthetics has been confusing and corrupting many of our writers for some time. We bear the intellectual yoke of the least sympathetic people, of the people that is, perhaps, least considerate of others, of the people that is least able to comprehend the sentiments and thoughts of other people, of the most proudly self-interested people.

There is no greater misrepresentation than the exoticism of the French writers who boast of being exotic. In the depth of his spirit, every Frenchman, however cultured he may be, believes that Shakespeare and Calderón are barbarians whose social function is to furnish raw material so that some Racine or other may construct definitive plays. When they judge a foreign author, their only sure, unchanging criterion is whether he is more or less Frenchified, whether he resembles them more or less. In this respect Zola, narrow-minded Zola, that man whose brain was as opinionated as his ignorance was great, was a model.

On the other hand, see what an evaluation of our most representative and most natural authors has come to us from England and Germany. It can be said that Schlegel introduced Calderón to the European public, as Schopenhauer did for Gracián, and perhaps the Quijote is nowhere better understood than in England. And Italy, the other great Latin nation, evidences a much deeper understanding of our spiritual life than France does.

One of the commonest complaints that the French make against us is that we talk too much. The only answer to this is: "What is wrong with talking?"

We could well take issue with their cold intellectualism. For that is the weakness of the classic French spirit—it is very cold and very intellectual. A race of great mathematicians and geometricians, whose pure art leads them to falsify even emotion.

If anyone wishes to take issue with me, I shall remind him at once of the statement that Africa begins with the Pyrenees, which was not made on this side of those mountains. I recalled this because I was thinking of a great African orator, that ardent, praiseworthy African, Augustín de Hipona. And it seems appropriate to compare the speech of the African bishop with the rhetoric of the French bishop, de Bossuet, and to believe that the first was an explorer and discoverer of the profundities of the human soul, and the second was merely an eloquent expounder, in the French style, of the great French commonplaces.

Sarmiento said in the description that he made of his trip to Spain in 1846, that when the classic French genre crossed the Pyrenees and arrived to ennoble the Spanish theatre, since the people could not understand its beauties, it abandoned the representations that were foreign to it, and was satisfied with the bullfights, where at least it was safe from the three unities, and where it could sense beauties that escaped the eyes of the classics. These beauties escape me too, and I ame not a classic of the French type, but I do not fail to grasp the correctness of the remark by the great Argentine, so deeply Spanish himself. Perhaps today the public is seeking refuge in the one-hour comic sketches, fleeing new French imitators, now that the last Spanish dramatist has lost his inspiration.

NATURALNESS

Of course, since nature is something that is constantly being formed, we must continually be working on our own temperament and seeking elsewhere elements with which to develop and improve it. But the better these elements are assimilated the more we shall profit by them, and we can best assimilate those that are in closest harmony with our nature. And the proximity, as well as the similarity of the languages has led us to seek nourishment for our spiritual development where it was perhaps least available. All those phrases such as "hyperborean fogs" and "Germanic echoes" reveal an erroneous understanding of the Spanish soul. The Latinity of Italy, so evident today, is mainly an imitation of German models.

I am sure that when they no longer read Zola and Maupassant in Spain, Dickens will still be read, and he will be more popular than they, to the extent that popularity belongs in this picture.

Here we would be faced with a new aspect of the problem; that is, the difference between European literature and world literature in general, and national literatures, and how authors that are very highly rated in national literatures pass almost unnoticed abroad, and conversely, how authors that at home are considered second- or even fifth-rate, achieve world-wide circulation.

The scale of values used by the experts in one country in judging its authors is radically changed as soon as the frontier is reached.

But this is a different and very interesting aspect that we must leave for another occasion.

The Song Of Eternal Waters

The narrow path, painfully hewn through solid stone, winds across the abyss. On the one hand huge boulders and rugged cliffs, and on the other the ceaseless murmur of the waters hidden in the murky depths of the abyss. From time to time the path widens into resting places, spots where a dozen travelers might rest above the abyss, sheltered by thatched roofs. In the distance a lofty castle on a towering crag stands out against the sky. Clouds are floating over it, torn by the loftiest spires.

Maquetas is among the pilgrims. In his hurried journey, he sees only the road before him and occasionally glimpses the castle. He is singing an old song learned from his grandmother in his infancy. His singing keeps him from hearing the prophetic murmur of the stream lost in the depths of the abyss.

As he reaches one of the resting places, a maiden calls to him from the grassy spot where she is sitting:

"Maquetas, stop a moment. Come here and rest by my side, with your back to the abyss. Let us talk a little. There is nothing like a few friendly words to give us strength for this journey. Stop a while with me. After you are rested and refreshed, you can again set out."

"I cannot, maiden," answers Maquetas, checking his step but without entirely stopping, "I cannot; the castle

154

is still far away, and I must get there before the sun sets behind its towers."

"You cannot lose anything by stopping a while, sir, because after a while you can start out again faster and with renewed strength. Aren't you tired?"

"Very tired, maiden."

"Then stop and rest. You have the grass to lie on and my lap for a pillow. What more could you ask for? Come on, stop."

And she stretches out her arms to him.

Maquetas stops a moment, and as he hesitates he hears the voice of the invisible current running in the depths of the abyss. He leaves the road, stretches out on the grass and puts his head in the lap of the maiden, who wipes the sweat from his forehead with her soft white hands, while he looks up at the morning sky, a sky that is young as the maiden's eyes are young.

"What are you singing, maiden?"

"I am not singing. It is the water there below, behind us."

"What is it singing?"

"It is singing the song of eternal rest. But rest now."

"Did you not just say that it is eternal?"

"The song of the torrent below is; but rest."

"And later. . . ."

"Rest, Maquetas, don't worry about 'later.' "

The maiden places a kiss upon his lips; Maquetas feels it dissolving and spreading throughout his body, and it and her sweetness fill him with heavenly pleasure. He swoons. He dreams that he is falling, falling ceaselessly into the fathomless chasm. When he awakens and opens his eyes, he sees the afternoon sky.

"Oh, maiden, how late it is! I no longer have time to reach the castle. Let me go, let me go."

"All right, go; may God be with you and guide you, and don't forget me, Maquetas."

"Kiss me once again."

"I shall, and may it give you strength."

With the kiss Maquetas feels himself strengthened a hundredfold and he begins to run on his way, singing as he goes. And he runs and runs, passing other pilgrims. One of them shouts as he passes:

"You will stop, Maquetas!"

Maquetas notices that the sun is beginning to set behind the castle and his heart feels a sudden chill. The glow of the sunset fills the sky for a moment; the clanking of the draw-bridge chains is heard. Maquetas whispers to himself:

"They are closing the castle."

Night comes creeping on, dark and fathomless. Soon Maquetas has to stop because he can see nothing at all; he is wrapped in darkness. Maquetas stops and is silent, and in the impenetrable darkness only the murmur of the waters of the current in the abyss is heard. The cold grows more intense.

Maquetas crouches, feels the road with his trembling hands, and, like a fox, goes cautiously forward on all fours. He is avoiding the chasm. He goes on thus for a long, long time. And he says to himself:

"Alas, that girl deceived me! Why did I listen to her?"

The cold becomes unbearable. Like a sword with a thousand points, it pricks him everywhere. Maquetas no longer feels the ground, or his hands, or his feet. Terrified, he stops. Or rather, he does not know whether he is stopped or going along on all fours.

Maquetas feels suspended in the midst of the darkness; blackness is all around. He hears only the ceaseless murmur of the waters in the abyss.

"I am going to cry out," Maquetas says to himself, and tries to shout. No sound is heard; it does not leave his chest; his voice seems frozen.

Then Maquetas thinks:

"Can I be dead?"

And as he thinks of this, he feels as if the cold and darkness are becoming solid, closing in around him forever.

"Can this be death?" Maquetas goes on thinking. "Must I live always thus, in pure thought and memory? What of the castle? And the abyss? What are those waters saying? What a dream; what an endless dream! Never to sleep! To die, thus, from sleep, ceaselessly, little by little, and never to be able to go to sleep. . . . And now, what am I going to do? What shall I do tomorrow?

"Tomorrow? What about tomorrow? What does tomorrow mean? What is this idea of tomorrow that comes to me out of the darkness, from where those waters are singing? Tomorrow! For me there is no tomorrow! All is now, all is blackness and cold. Even the song of the eternal waters seems frozen, one single prolonged note.

"Did I really die? How slowly the dawn comes! But I do not know how much time has passed since the sun set behind the castle towers. . . .

"There was once," he goes on thinking, "a man named Maquetas, a valiant traveler, who was journeying daily

157

toward a castle where a meal was awaiting him by the fire, and, after the meal, a good bed for his rest, and on the bed a good mate. And there, in the castle, he was to live forever, listening to endless stories, finding solace in his mate, in perpetual youth. And the days were to be all alike and calm. And as they were passing, forgetfulness would gradually encompass them. And all those days would gradually become one eternal day, one day eternally renewed, a perpetual day treasuring an infinite number of yesterdays and an infinite number of tomorrows.

"And that Maquetas thought that that was life and started out upon his journey. On he went, stopping at inns, where he slept, and each time that the sun rose again, once more he started upon his way. And once, as he was leaving an inn one morning, he came across an old beggar sitting upon a tree trunk by the door, who asked him, 'Maquetas, what is the meaning of things?' And, shrugging his shoulders, that Maquetas answered, 'What do I care?' And the old beggar again spoke, asking, 'What is the meaning of this road?' This time Maquetas answered, slightly impatiently, 'Why do you ask me what the road means? Do you suppose that I know? Does anyone know? Does the road have any meaning? Don't bother me, and God be with you!' The old beggar frowned and smiled sadly as he looked at the ground.

"And after a while that Maquetas came to a very rough region and had to cross a wild range of mountains by a very steep path hewn in the stone above an abyss in whose depths the waters of an invisible torrent were singing. There, in the distance, he glimpsed the castle at which he was going to arrive before sunset, and when he saw it he felt his heart jump with sudden joy, and he quickened his step. But a maiden, pretty as a dream, made him stop and rest a while on the grass, holding his head in her lap, and that Maquetas halted. And as he was saying goodbye the maiden gave him a kiss, the kiss of death, and as the sun sank behind the castle towers, that Maquetas was encircled by cold and darkness which grew thicker and thicker and became solid. And there was silence broken only by the song of the eternal waters in the abyss, for there, in life, the sounds, the voices, the songs, and the murmurs rose from a vague murmuring, from a vibrant mist, but here this song flowed from the depth of the silence, from the silence of darkness and cold, from the silence of death.

"Of death? Of death, yes, because that Maquetas, the valiant traveler, died.

"What a charming story and how sad! It is much more charming and much sadder than that old song that my grandmother taught me. Let's see, I am going to repeat it again. . . .

"There was once a man named Maquetas, a valiant traveler, whose name was Maquetas, who was journeying daily toward a castle. . . ."

And, again, and again, and again, Maquetas repeated the story of that Maquetas and he is still repeating it, and he will keep on repeating it as long as the eternal waters of the invisible stream keep on singing in the abyss, and these waters will go on singing forever, and forever, and forever, knowing no yesterday or tomorrow, forever, forever, forever. . . .

To A Young Writer

My young friend, we cannot understand each other; you speak one language and I another, and we both refuse to translate our terms. Just to hear from mechanical lips the kind of phrases that you employ, makes them unintelligible to me.

One of them is the way you use "arrive." Its meaning is becoming less and less clear. Please explain these: "So-and-so has arrived," "John Doe will never arrive," "Today it is very very difficult for a young man to arrive," and other expressions of the same sort. What is this business about arriving? Arrive where? There is but one certain and infallible arrival, that of death. And perhaps that is better termed a departure.

Ulysses was once relating to the daughter of the king of the Phaeacians how he met Iphimedia among the shades of the dead heroines in the kingdom of Hades. She had given birth to two sons, Otus and Ephialtes, who, at the age of nine, were nine cubits broad and nine fathoms tall, and, excepting only Orion, were the most beautiful sons that Mother Earth had ever produced. These two young giants threatened to declare war on the immortals themselves, and in preparation for it, they attempted to put Mount Ossa on Olympus and Pelion on Ossa, so that they might climb to the sky. And they would have succeeded, added Ulysses, had they been older. But Apollo killed them before the down of adolescence appeared on their faces.

Are you trying, my young friend, to reach the sky heaping mountain on mountain? Are you afraid of dying before you reach the prudence of spiritual youth? If this is the case, I understand your use of "arrive," if this is not true, I do not understand it.

Woe to you on the day when you do arrive! Then will the return begin.

This is why I have so often wanted you to have hopes that you will neither regret nor realize, hopes ever green that never bear fruit, hopes in the eternal bloom of hope.

You do not enjoy being discussed and contradicted. Alas for you, if you were not! On the day when you become a successful writer, recognized and understood by all, on the day when those who now discuss you, or their children, bow down to you in reverence—if you see that unhappy day — then will your soul be in its old age. When Dante was exploring the kingdoms of the dead, they were surprised to see that he cast a shadow and by that they knew that he was alive. If he had not cast it, he would already have passed through the portal of death, where every shadow is lost in the darkness. On the day when you no longer cast a shadow, you will have entered the kingdom of the immortals, you will be dead.

Yes, I know that you long to enter this realm of empty dreams, the immortality of death. But, do you really believe that the prey is worth the hunt, that the victory is worth the fight?

If you wound a man, and he cries out, you are living; if he does not stir, one or the other of you is dead. Probably both.

On the day when they triumphantly say of you, "I understand this man!" you are lost; for, henceforth, you are not yours but theirs. From then on you will always tell them what they thought you were going to tell them and what they wanted you to tell them.

Neither do I entirely understand, except piecemeal, what you are seeking. Please tell me.

God keep you from thinking that your success is complete. From that moment your decline will begin. There is a Latin word which means ended, entirely done, finished; it is *perfectus,* perfect. Beware of perfection!

It is true that we were told to be perfect as our Father in heaven is perfect; but the Gospels are full of paradoxes and that is one of them. In fact, the paradox, together with the parable and the metaphor, were Christ's favorite ways of teaching. And he set for us an ideal of unapproachable perfection, the only force that can move us to strive to accomplish what we can. We cannot arrive at divine perfection, and it is precisely for this reason that such a goal was set for us.

You will probably tell me that the purpose of this goal was for one to know himself and for no other reason, and you will remind me of that very famous and often misquoted Delphic saying. I do not know whether knowing oneself is the beginning or end of wisdom, and the end of wisdom, like every ending, is a terrible thing. But I think that it might be better to change the famous maxim, saying, "Study thyself." Study yourself, whether or not you come to know yourself, and perhaps it will be better if you do not, provided that you study. The more you study, the more you will broaden and deepen yourself spiritually, and the more you broaden and deepen yourself, the more difficult it will be to know yourself.

Study yourself while you are working, in your work, in whatever you do, outside of yourself. It is very bad to keep probing your conscience alone and in the dark. In the light of day and in full view, expose it to the sun and open air.

Once before I told you to consider the matter of personal diaries, and you didn't understand me. Personal diaries are the enemies of personal privacy. They destroy it. More than one individual who has begun to keep a personal diary, began by writing down what he felt, and ended by feeling, in order to write it down. He would get up every morning wondering what he was going to put down in his diary that night, and whatever he said or did, his diary was always before him. And so the man came to belong to the diary, and it gradually ceased to be the diary of a man.

That is the trouble with every narrow interest. They say that in organic chemical analysis it sometimes happens that when they attempt to study a very unstable and complicated compound, it is destroyed by the reagent and, instead of the body they are seeking to study and understand, they find the products of its decomposition. The same is true of psychological analysis. This is why in most of the so-called psychological novels we find descriptions of states of conscience, but almost never do we come across souls, complete, natural souls, like those that we can sense moving and breathing behind the poorly constructed psychology of the novels. To see oneself, a mirror is better than to close one's eyes and look within.

Are you anxious to give yourself a personal touch? Fine, but what personal touch shall be yours? Do you know yourself, by any chance? Does the one who is speaking know best the quality of his voice? The appearance of a river depends on the bed and the banks. Let yourself go at the will of your current, jumping over dams, and worry no more. Thus one gets to the sea and the river is made.

. . . .

I have something more to say to you, I hardly know what, but remember that I realize how futile it is to advise anyone, especially youths. As a professor I am quite aware of the old maxim, "I sell advice to young and old, but when I need it, I find it's sold."

Someone else might be disturbed on being asked for advice, as I have been asked by you this time. But I well know that when a young man asks for advice, he is almost never sincere, and is really seeking something else. The request for advice is but a pretext. And more than once I have been disdainfully attacked, because I did not say what it was hoped and expected that I would say. Nobody should be blamed for not living up to a false concept of himself that others have formed.

I warn you in advance that few things will disappoint you more in your career than the discovery that you will be esteemed most for the things that you cherish least in yourself, and that you will be scorned on account of the qualities that you hold most dear. The former Jesuit and Catholic priest, Jorge Tyrrell, whose growing fame will make itself heard among us, says in his *Lex Credendi* these gloomy words:

"What is more sad and depressing in our own experience than to be loved and admired for qualities that we know that we do not have, or for those that we would prefer not to possess, while, on the contrary, what we believe to be the best in us passes unnoticed?"

Observe that in this melancholy passage Tyrrell says, "to be loved and admired." What a contrast between those two! At your age you are probably more interested in the admiration than the affection of others. You would likely desire the first even at the expense of the second, but the day will come, my young friend, when your soul will thirst for affection. You will yearn to be loved and, when that time comes, may God free you from the most excruciating of all spiritual torments, that of being unable to love in return. It is sad not to be loved, but it is sadder not to be able to love. And there are souls that want to love and cannot, the victims of a racking, burning, shriveling drought.

. . . .

Have I anything further to say to you? There must be something, doubtless, but it does not come to me. As usual, I am leaving unsaid what I wanted to say most. As has often been repeated, our best thoughts are those that die without our having succeeded in formulating them. And it is just barely possible that the best thing about us is what others say, or we make them say, about us. My thoughts germinate in me and bear fruit in others.